The Power of
**Spiritual
Intelligence**

The Power of
Spiritual
Intelligence

Tony Buzan

Thorsons

Thorsons
An Imprint of HarperCollins*Publishers*
77–85 Fulham Palace Road
Hammersmith, London W6 8JB

The Thorsons website address is: www.thorsons.com

First published 2001

10 9 8 7 6 5 4

© Tony Buzan 2001

Tony Buzan asserts the moral right to be
identified as the author of this work

Mind-Maps® is a registered trade mark of the Buzan Group

Plate section illustrations by Alan Burton

A catalogue record for this book
is available from the British Library

ISBN 0 7225 4047 7

Printed and bound in Great Britain by
Martins the Printers Ltd, Berwick upon Tweed

dedication

The Power of Spiritual Intelligence is fondly and warmly dedicated to Lesley and Teri Bias; my Mum, Jean Buzan; Lorraine Gill, Vanda North, Nicky and Strilli Oppenheimer, Dr Petite Rao, Caroline Shott and Carole Tonkinson for their spiritual help in my personal life and for their dedication and hard work in making both this little book and giant dream come true.

contents

list of mind-maps®

Summary Mind-Map® of Chapter 1. This Mind-Map® summarizes how an awareness of the 'Big Picture' – of our place in the universe, the fragility of the planet and how humankind can affect our world – is an important part of Spiritual Intelligence.

Summary Mind-Map® of Chapter 3. Life vision and purpose are summarized in this Mind-Map®, which shows how important goals are and how they can be reinforced through exercises.

Summary Mind-Map® of Chapter 5, in which the main themes of charity and gratitude are summarized, together with the benefits that giving and receiving bring to you and to others.

Summary Mind-Map® of Chapter 6. This Mind-Map® summarizes the theme of laughter, depicting how humour can help overcome the most adverse of circumstances, and can bring you a longer, healthier and less stressed life.

Summary Mind-Map® of Chapter 7. The Mind-Map® of the Child's Playground summarizes the wonderful way children look at the world, and how we too can rediscover a child*like* attitude to life.

Summary Mind-Map® of Chapter 8. The power of Ritual is summarized in this Mind-Map®, with branches showing the benefits of having regular rituals, how the repetition of rituals reinforces them and the Spiritual Workout exercises to help introduce Ritual into your life.

Summary Mind-Map® of Chapter 9. This Mind-Map® shows how you can create moments of peace through meditation, 'time-outs' and 'sanctuary breaks' to unclutter your mind and promote well-being.

Summary Mind-Map® of Chapter 10. This Mind-Map® summarizes the power of love to overcome every obstacle, and how love is the key to awareness, compassion and Spiritual Intelligence.

acknowledgements

Gratitude and thanks again to my top-of-the-bestseller-lists *Head First* team who have done it once again with *The Power of Spiritual Intelligence*! To my Commissioning Editor, Carole Tonkinson; my Editor, Charlotte Ridings; my artist and illustrator, Alan Burton; Paul Redhead; Toby Watson; Tim Burn; Yvette Cowles; Jo Lal; Megan Slyfield; Jacqui Caulton; Aislinn McCormick; and our new team member, Ariel Kahn. Thank you once again for standing 'on the shoulders of giants' – your own!

journey to paradise

introduction

**We are not human beings
having a spiritual experience;
we are spiritual beings
having a human experience.**

(Teilhard de Chardin)

Are you a spiritual person? Many people confuse being spiritual with being religious, but they are very different things. When you are Spiritually Intelligent you become more aware of the 'big picture' – for yourself and the universe, and your place and purpose in it.

Spiritual Intelligence is considered by many to be the most important of our many intelligences, and has the power to transform your life, civilization, the planet and the course of history. In *The Power of Spiritual Intelligence* I will explore the nature of spirituality, and show you how you can develop this wonderful intelligence. You will be able to develop your personal values – concepts like truth and honesty – and become involved first in understanding and knowing more of yourself, and then reaching out to participate in and help the community at large.

Happily, developing your Spiritual Intelligence will allow you to see the lighter and more humorous side of things, and to regain those qualities such as enthusiasm, cheerfulness, energy and persistence that characterize children. Not only that – I will show you how you can increase your inner peace and strength, and so become better able to control and reduce the stresses that often blight our modern, busy lives.

First, I would like to tell you about my own spiritual career, and how I came to realize that there was such a thing as Spiritual Intelligence.

Two stories tell the tale:

Story 1: Chocolate Bars, Purity of Soul and Bribery!

When I was a young teenager, I began to ask 'the big questions' such as what is the meaning of life? Why is there so much suffering in the world? Do animals have emotions? Why do we die? What's the point of being honest or good? Are there other planets with life on them? How big is the universe and where does it end? And so on. My friends and I thought we might get some answers by going to the church Sunday School, so this we dutifully did.

Our Sunday School teacher was a bullying, arrogant man, with a domineering and authoritarian style. One Sunday he said to us that if we brought in new recruits to the Sunday School the following week, he would give us a chocolate bar for every new person brought in.

My hand immediately shot up! I pointed out to the teacher that he had, in a previous lesson, talked about purity of soul and the evils of bribery. Should we not, if we were truly spiritual, bring people to the Sunday School because we wanted to help them on their paths? Should we not, therefore, do it purely for the love of the other person? Should we not do it with pleasure, enthusiasm and generosity, expecting no reward whatsoever? By offering us all chocolate bars, was he not, in fact, bribing us?!

I was told never to ask such questions again, and to leave the class for rudeness and insubordination!

I never returned, and decided from that point on that anything to do with spirituality was either a con, irrelevant or wimpish, and that logic and argument were a far more 'true path'.

Story 2: Logic versus Spirituality

By the time I was 20 and at university, I had hardened my views on the supremacy of logic and the weakness of spirituality and emotion, while becoming a confirmed atheist. I had honed my verbal and logical reasoning skills and relished a good intellectual argument! Imagine my delight when my doorbell rang one day, and a frail, middle-aged lady announced that she had come to try to save my soul!

Like a spider preparing to ensnare a fly, I invited her in to let her explain her views on the need for me to be more spiritually aware. By this time I had become well-versed in the history of philosophy and the great debates on morality, God, and the meaning of life. In less than 15 minutes I had this gentle lady floundering but, to my surprise, still upbeat and unbowed.

She explained that helping other people was a relatively new direction in her life, a life which had known a lot of pain and suffering, and which was now much more beautiful and calm. She cheerfully asked if she could come back next week with someone more experienced in the field, and I agreed, anticipating another logic battle, with a more 'worthy' opponent.

A week later she duly returned, proudly introducing me to a young man who had just graduated from university and who was extremely knowledgeable in the field. We immediately locked horns, and a great intellectual tussle took place. Finally, after an hour, he made one fatal logical mistake, and I pounced. The victory was mine!

Still unbowed, the lady asked if she could return the following week with one of the most senior members of her organization. Once again I said yes.

On the day of the next meeting, a snowstorm had blown up, and it was bitterly cold. Nevertheless, my Angel of Mercy was there. She introduced me, with pride and respect, to her companion: a middle-aged man who looked like a character out of a cheap gangster movie, who was a very senior person in her organization. He appeared to be the opposite of everything that spirituality stood for, knew little about ethical or moral arguments, and seemed intent only on raising money from me and parading his status. I accused him of ignorance, greed and dishonesty and had him red-faced and speechless within five minutes.

Another great victory!

This, however, was soon to turn to dust. When the pair left, the lady looked up at me with a fractured face, her expression one of failure, disillusionment, loss, pleading and an almost unbearable pain. As I closed the door on her forever, those same feelings surged through me.

What had I done?

This gentle lady had spent several weeks of her life preparing for and meeting me, with the sole purpose of helping to save my soul. And what had I done to express my thanks and gratitude for this totally unselfish gesture on my behalf? Beaten her with the truncheons of logic and words; humiliated and demeaned those she loved and respected in front of her; attempted to destroy the foundations of a newly structured, innocent and loving life; and after gloating at my 'triumphs', had turned her out into the snow. I sat down, stunned at the horror of what I had just done. Logic and words suddenly seemed irrelevant, and my whole being was overwhelmed with sorrow and remorse.

Without knowing it, my Angel of Mercy had more than accomplished her task and, in the final analysis, had won her argument hands down and spirit up! Wherever you are, dear lady, I eternally thank you for your wonderful and successful rescue mission!

In one flash of heart-rending realization, my life had been changed. I came to see that there was more to intelligence than simply words, numbers and logic. (In fact, I was soon to discover that there were multiple intelligences – Creative, Personal, Social, Sensual, Physical, Sexual, Spatial and Spiritual, as well as Verbal and Numerical, which I explore in my book *Head First*.)

spiritual intelligence – a definition

We often hear of:

- 'the *spirit* of the age'
- 'full of *spirits*'
- people in 'poor' or 'high *spirits*'
- 'troubled *spirits*'
- 'the nation's *spirit*'
- 'my *spiritual* father'
- 'she was a leading *spirit*...'
- 'my *spiritual* home'

but just what are 'spirit' and 'spiritual'?

The whole concept of spirit comes from the Latin *spiritus*, meaning breath. The modern term refers to your life energy and to the 'non-physical' part of you, including your emotions and character. It includes your vital qualities of energy, enthusiasm, courage and determination. (It is interesting to note that spirit also means a form of purified alcohol. Note that the emphasis is on *purified*!)

Your Spiritual Intelligence is concerned with how you grow and develop these qualities. It is also concerned with the protection and development of your soul, which the Oxford English Dictionary defines as your 'moral and emotional identity' and the intensity of its 'emotional and intellectual energy'.

Spiritual Intelligence progresses naturally from your Personal Intelligence (knowledge, appreciation and understanding of yourself), through Social Intelligence (knowledge, appreciation and understanding of other people), to the appreciation and understanding of all other life forms and the Universe itself. In fact, contact with, understanding, and an appreciation of nature is a major aspect in the development of your Spiritual Intelligence.

Self-actualization

Self-actualization is the ultimate state of achievement described by the respected American psychologist Abraham Maslow, in what he described as his *Hierarchy of Needs*. Maslow discovered that, regardless of what tribe or place on the planet they were from, all human beings went through ascending stages of survival and spiritual development. These included:

- the need for food
- the need for shelter
- the need for physical health
- the need for family
- the need for education
- the need for social integration
- the need for intellectual, social and material accomplishment.

It is only when all these are met that people reached their ultimate stage of human development: *Self-actualization*.

Maslow defined self-actualization as a spiritual state, in which the individual poured out creativity, was playful, joyful, tolerant, with a sense of purpose and a mission to help others to achieve this state of wisdom and bliss. All of these are to be accomplished in an environment of growing compassion and love.

Maslow was describing what we now call Spiritual Intelligence!

the global hunger for spiritual intelligence

The new global emphasis on developing the power of Spiritual Intelligence has come at just the right time for a world that is often described as spiritually sick.

'What is the world coming to?' we ask, when words like 'divine' are downgraded to describe, breathlessly, new furniture or clothes; when people describe themselves as 'transported' when their suburban gardens are given makeovers by TV experts; and when 'ecstasy' is used to describe not a state of transcendence, but a cheap and brain-damaging drug?

However, all is not as bad as it seems – the very fact that people are looking for 'that buzz' confirms that the spirit is still alive! It is simply looking for guidance to find the right path, and has momentarily lost its way among the mundane and commonplace.

Even the incessant stream of bad news which daily pours out of our radios, our TVs and the papers contains some silver linings. Natural disasters like earthquakes, avalanches and floods cause undeniably awful pain and suffering; but similarly they can result in extraordinary displays of compassion and community of spirit. Such events often help jolt us out of the semi-robotic way in which we allow our lives to run, and into a new awareness that is out of the ordinary. This is an awareness and insight that can be brought about also by birth and death, loss of loved ones, a sunrise, a painting, and all those things that have inspired the greatest art, poetry and music throughout the centuries.

There is more good news!

More and more people in affluent societies are growing tired of the shallowness of their materialistic lives, and are searching for a new set of values by which to live; values which emphasize a new sense of collective belonging to and responsibility for a world that is in an increasingly fragile state.

A recent survey conducted by John Naisbitt, the author of *Megatrends 2000*, showed that for the first time in history more people were moving from the big cities to the suburbs; from the suburbs to the exurbs; and from the exurbs back to the countryside than were moving into the cities.

Why? Because, people reported, they felt that in some way they were 'losing their souls' and that they needed to get back in touch with themselves, with Nature, and with the sense of human community for which they longed. They wanted more Quality of Life; a life that fed, rather than depleted their spirits.

At the same time, the world is experiencing a new Renaissance. In country after country, more art galleries, concert halls and museums are being built. And in many countries more people than ever before are studying (professionally and for personal enjoyment) music, drawing, painting, creative writing, theatre and dance.

You are living, at the beginning of this 21st Century of the Brain and the Millennium of the Mind, in a world that is transforming itself from a relatively 'dark night of the soul' to an age of Spiritual awareness, development and enlightenment. *You* are part of that process.

'Great men are they who see that the spiritual is stronger than any material force.'

(Ralph Waldo Emerson)

Case History – Valentina Tereshkova

Many leading individuals are publicly calling for greater attention to be paid to Spiritual Intelligence and a more caring and nurturing approach toward the children of the future and the planet. One particularly notable example is Dr Valentina Tereshkova. On 16 June 1963, a powerful rocket boosted the space capsule 'Vostok 6' into outer space and Valentina piloted it 48 orbits around the earth. Three days later she landed her space capsule safely, and became and remains the only woman in the world to accomplish solo flight into space. She received many awards and decorations, and has devoted an increasing part of her time to speaking at international peace conferences. She was recently nominated for the Women of the Year award of 'The Woman of the 20th Century', and in her acceptance speech she stressed the responsibility we all have for the future of human civilization:

'We all have to understand and in full measure accept our responsibility for the future of human civilisation in all areas of activity – in the economy, in science and culture and art … I believe we all know which dangers we have in mind. The pollution of the environment due to the retroactivity of men, the pollution of outer space, and the problem of the sensible use of the scientific and technological achievements [for] the benefit and not the detriment of humanity.

'Another problem is to protect the spiritual health of our children, to provide them with a moral compass to choose the right road in the limitless cyber space. Can we solve all these problems? Yes we can, thanks to responsibility and solidarity.'

The recent Olympics 2000 in Sydney, Australia give a vivid illustration of the benefits and effects of people using their Spiritual Intelligence. For two weeks 17 million people overcame the most horrendous logistical problems, put aside personal considerations in order to care for others, handled all kinds of stress, and in four million individual cases, volunteered their time, money and energy to celebrate human achievement. Commentators from around the world were 'gob smacked' at the sight and sound of people forming spontaneous choirs on trains, boats and airplanes; of everyone helping everyone else; and of the continuous, almost hypnotic spirit of cheerfulness and playfulness that pervaded the entire country.

This was an example of an entire country, itself composed of many races, religions and creeds, hosting those from the entire planet and succeeding, miraculously, in creating a momentary paradise-on-earth.

Case History – Diana, Princess of Wales

The shared outpouring of public grief at the death of Diana, Princess of Wales in 1997 was seen by some as a worrying manifestation of the power of celebrity and how the emptiness of some people's lives led them to attach themselves to popular icons, living their lives vicariously through them. While that is one way of looking at it, there is a more Spiritually Intelligent view of the events – that people overcame their differences to share their grief for a woman who had done so much to help others through her charity work that she had become a symbol of hope and compassion.

Diana will be remembered by millions the world over for her

---

high-profile stand on the use of land mines, and her compassion for AIDS patients. Although she suffered personal problems, she reached out to others in greater need and, by her example, she inspired others to do likewise.

Far from 'going to hell in a hand-basket', the world in which you live is undergoing a wonderful period of spiritual growth. This spiritual power that you, your family, friends and all of us have, is infinite. This book is designed to help you tap into that power, and to use it for your own and others' good.

'We cannot teach people anything; we can only help them discover it within themselves.'

(Galileo Galilei)

the power of spiritual intelligence – an overview

The ten chapters of *The Power of Spiritual Intelligence* deal with the 'Ten Graces' that combine to form Spiritual Intelligence.

Chapter 1 – Getting the 'Big Picture'

In this chapter I will demonstrate to you that you are a miracle, and you will learn some incredible facts about you and your relationship with the universe. Each one of us has a tangible effect and impact on history, and you will read the thoughts of some of the world's greatest thinkers about yourself, about your amazing capacities, and about your power.

Chapter 2 – Exploring Your Values

Your values and principles determine your behaviour, and have a massive effect on the probability of your success in life. By applying the lessons you will learn, you will, literally, improve your own and your friends' chances of survival! In this chapter I shall explore the establishment and development of these principles, and will introduce you to thoughts of Buddha, Muhammad and others on this subject.

Chapter 3 – Your Life Vision and Purpose

In Chapter 3 you will be introduced to the power of your vision and your ability to plan. By applying this power you will be able to transform your life for the better. For this purpose I will provide you with a special technique that I have used to help Olympic athletes, business people, and tens of thousands of others world-wide who were seeking to increase their probability of success.

With a clear and defined purpose, your life will gain meaning and direction, and you will become healthier, stronger and more confident.

Chapter 4 – Compassion: Understanding Yourself and Others

Chapter 4 will explore further the 'Amazing You'. I will show you games and exercises that will demonstrate to you how creative and unique you are. These same exercises will reveal to you all the spiritual qualities you share in common with the rest of humanity.

You will also be introduced to the thoughts of great spiritual leaders on compassion and understanding such as Gandhi, and the reflections of John Donne, Muhammad Ali, Nelson Mandela and Ralph Waldo Emerson. Each of these will help you develop your own Compassion and Understanding.

Chapter 5 – Give and Receive! Charity and Gratitude

When you learn the twin graces of Charity and Gratitude, you multiply your Spiritual Intelligence several-fold. Your soul learns to breathe in (gratitude) and to breathe out (charity). One of the richest men of the 19th century, Andrew Carnegie, is a wonderful example of these qualities.

By applying the lessons of this chapter, you will become spiritually stronger and healthier, while at the same time becoming more nurturing, gentle and kind.

Chapter 6 – The Power of Laughter

Laughter is a vital quality of Spiritual Intelligence, and benefits you in many ways, including reducing stress levels and generally leading to a more cheerful and happier life. Research also demonstrates that laughter can help you live a longer and healthier life. You should end this chapter one 'happy bunny'!

Chapter 7 – Onward to the Child's Playground

How can it be beneficial to become like a child again? You will find out in this chapter! Investigations have shown that the more Spiritually Intelligent you become, the more the childlike qualities of innocence, cheerfulness, joyfulness, spontaneity, enthusiasm and adventure increase in your life.

Chapter 8 – The Power of Ritual

How do you improve your spiritual and emotional stability, reduce your stress, become more persistent and determined and, as a result, stronger and more confident?

Is there a magic formula? Yes! It's called ritual, and in this chapter you will learn some important lessons from Indian Yogis. You will finish the chapter knowing how to create your own rituals, and appreciating the incredible effect they have on your brain, body and spirit.

Chapter 9 – Peace

The modern world can provide a lot of 'negative vibes' – accumulated stress, jangled nerves and mental clutter. For your survival, both spiritual and otherwise, it is essential to learn techniques to reduce and to eliminate stress, and to cultivate an internal environment that is calm, tranquil and serene. In this chapter I will guide you, with the help of the Maharishi and Confucius, among others, toward that state in which you will be free from mental disturbance, anxiety and distress.

Chapter 10 – All You Need Is Love!

In this final chapter you will be introduced to the ultimate power – the Power of Love. You will read stories of adventure, trial and tribulation, death and hope, and will be given techniques and approaches to ease suffering, pain and despair.

■   ■   ■

The Power of Spiritual Intelligence is designed to be stimulating, informative, practical and fun. Each chapter comprises: a definition of each 'Grace' or quality being described, and how it will benefit you in your day-to-day life; stories to inspire and guide you in developing your Spiritual Intelligence; and words of wisdom to give you good food for your spiritual thought. There are also Spiritual Workouts in each chapter, with practical games and advice to help you strengthen the particular aspect of Spiritual Intelligence being discussed.

An additional feature is Spiritual Intelligence 'Spirit Boosters', to increase the power of the workouts, which take the form of 'Intentions' and 'Affirmations' that you can repeat to yourself on a regular basis. They will help you refine and strengthen your purpose in life, and by repetition, will reinforce these synaptic connections in your brain, thus increasing your mental and spiritual power.

The Spirit Boosters have been carefully worded to protect you from the many pitfalls that 'false positive thinking' can get you into. Their purpose is to keep:

- your body grounded
- your mind clear
- your soul rooted
- your energy flowing
- your Spiritual Intelligence and your life continuously enhanced.

The Power of Spiritual Intelligence also includes Mind-Maps®
– colourful, graphic learning tools that I have spent my life
developing. They are brilliant route-maps for the memory, allowing
you to organize facts and thoughts in such a way that the brain's
natural way of working is engaged right from the start. Within the
chapters there will be examples of and reference to Mind-Maps®,
as well as exercises in which Mind-Maps® will be used to enhance
and develop your Spiritual Intelligence.

By following the ideas contained in this book, you will be able to
enhance and develop your Spiritual Intelligence. To give you some idea
of your progress along your spiritual path, try answering the following
questions; and then come back to them when you have finished the book!

1   Do you feel 'at one' with nature? YES/NO
2   Are you playful? YES/NO
3   Do people consider you childlike (not child*ish*)? YES/NO
4   Do you like children? Do they respond truly to you? YES/NO
5   Are you known to be sympathetic to the problems of others?
    YES/NO
6   Do people come to you for help with personal, ethical or spiritual
    problems? YES/NO
7   Do you enjoy all kinds of weather? YES/NO
8   Do you dislike many kinds of weather (cold, heat, rain)? YES/NO
9   Do you like animals? Do they respond truly to you? YES/NO
10 Do you go out of your way to kill flies, bugs and 'creepie
    crawlies'? YES/NO

11   Do you believe honesty is the best policy? YES/NO

12   Do you believe the human race has a true purpose? YES/NO

13   Do you believe charity and charitable work is only for 'do-gooders'? YES/NO

14   Do you often experience feelings of awe and wonder? YES/NO

15   Do you have moments of great joy? YES/NO

16   Do you have feelings of oneness with all round you? YES/NO

17   Do you regularly pray or meditate? YES/NO

18   Do questions about the purpose of life, the nature of good and evil, and the relationship of humans to the universe intrigue or excite you? YES/NO

19   Do you like the 'sound of silence'? YES/NO

20   Do you care for our planet? YES/NO

21   Do you love yourself? YES/NO

22   Do you pick up your rubbish? YES/NO

23   Do you feel there is an individual or some power/energy greater than you? YES/NO

24   Are you hopeful? YES/NO

25   Are you enthusiastic? YES/NO

26   Are you compassionate? YES/NO

27   Are you grateful for your life? YES/NO

28   Are you respectful and considerate of others? YES/NO

29   Are you creative? YES/NO

getting the 'big picture'

chapter one

'Men go abroad to wonder at the height of mountains, at the huge waves of the sea, at the long courses of the rivers, at the vast compass of the oceans, at the circular motion of the stars; and they pass by themselves without wondering.'

(St. Augustine)

The first principle of Spiritual Intelligence is the realization that you are a miracle and are wonderful! There is no doubt about it, and you should hold yourself, *and others*, in awe. Each one of us is more precious, valuable, rare, beautiful and priceless than the most precious and rare ruby or diamond.

A miracle is defined as any 'amazing or wonderful' thing or event, or 'a person or thing that is a marvellous example of something' – as in 'a miracle of design'. The word 'miracle' derives from the Latin *miraculum*, a wonder, or wonderful thing. You cannot argue – all the evidence supports the fact that *you are* amazing. Consider the miracle of your own engineering:

- your body is made up of 200 intricately sculptured and mechanically perfect bones; 500 muscles with billions of muscle fibres, and seven miles-worth of nerve fibres to keep it all co-ordinated
- your eyes, ears, nose, skin and mouth are each so sensitive and complex that scientists are at a loss to explain how they all work, let alone replicate their functions adequately
- your heart is the most amazing mechanical pump yet devised, beating an average of 36 million times every single year of your life
- your brain contains a million, *million* brain cells – equivalent to 167 times the population of the planet – each single one of which is more powerful than the standard personal computers we are relying on more and more!

We also know that you are more unique and more different from each other person on earth than any snowflake is from its fellows.

Moreover, we know that the atoms of which you are made come from the stars. You are, in the very real sense of the word, a Starchild!

Each one of us is capable of the most amazing feats of courage, endurance, heroism and sacrifice, as well, unfortunately, as the worst excesses of greed, selfishness, depravity and cruelty – this is the miracle of being human.

**'Be humble for you are made of earth.
Be noble for you are made of stars.'**

(Serbian Proverb)

the bigger picture

A common activity for young children all over the planet, who are just beginning to explore the wider dimensions of their world, is to send a letter to a friend or pen pal, addressing it as follows:

My friend Jane Fitzgerald,
16 Paradise Street,
London,
England,
Europe,
The World,
The Milky Way,
The Universe.

These children are beginning to sense, as the Spiritually Intelligent do, that the universe is their home, and that they live in a series of bigger and bigger neighbourhoods.

It is the universe's vastness that creates a sense of excitement, wonder and awe, and which raises all kinds of spiritual questions about the meaning of our existence, and our individual place and significance in that universe.

**'Every now and then,
Take a good look at something
Not made with hands;
A mountain, a star,
The curve of a stream.
There will come to you
Wisdom and patience,
And above all, the assurance
That you are not alone in the world.'**

(Sidney Lovett)

And this universe *is* vast:

- our Earth is just one of the nine planets in our solar system that circles our sun
- our sun is tens of thousands times bigger than our Earth, and yet is only a small example of the *ten thousand million* suns that make up our local galaxy, on the edge of which we spin
- our galaxy is one of a *million million* galaxies, each one millions of light years across, and each one separated on average by a distance so great that if you travelled at the speed of light for 100 years you would still not bridge the gap!

Imagine how many atoms (the building blocks of all matter) there must be in the Universe, when just *one grain* of sand from many of the

the power of spiritual intelligence

hundreds of thousands of beaches on our small planet contains *millions* of atoms.

Spiritually Intelligent people actively cultivate an awareness of the magnificence of every living thing and the vast and gigantic beauty of the universe. This awareness has been furthered dramatically by the invention of telescopes and space probes and, of course, manned space flights. Thanks to these instruments, exquisitely beautiful pictures of planets, stars, galaxies and inter-galactic clouds where stars are born, trillions of miles above us, have been beamed directly into our televisions and living rooms. This dawning Spiritual awareness is beautifully encapsulated in the story of astronaut Edgar Mitchell.

I met Edgar Mitchell in 1973, a couple of years after he had flown to and around the moon on the Apollo 14 mission. His experiences had radically changed his life, and he had established an institute for the study of humanity and the environment. He told the following story:

The Astronaut's Story

The training at NASA for the flight to and around the moon was very, very, thorough. The astronauts had simulated every stage of the flight in terms of duration and daily activities – they had literally 'gone to the moon and back' while on Earth!

Indeed the training had been *so* thorough that Mitchell reported virtually no emotions of fear or exaltation when they took off, because it felt so familiar and 'normal'.

This familiarity continued all the way to the moon, everything running smoothly, on schedule and, as far as the crew were concerned, almost robot-like. They arrived and began to prepare for their journey to the 'dark side of the moon'.

This, like everything else, had been rehearsed. The trip was to take only an hour or so. The significant thing about being on the dark side of the moon was that for the first time on the journey, the sight of the earth would be totally blocked from view, and no radio or television waves could either penetrate or go round the moon. The astronauts would be *totally* excommunicated from Earth!

Mitchell said that the first five minutes on the dark side were fine, but after that the simulation training began to peel away, and concern, a touch of fear, and his imagination began to kick in. He began to think more and more about Earth – about his wife and children, his home, his neighbourhood, his friends and the places they met, and the changing colours of the seasons.

As his imagination expanded, time began to stretch, as it does when you are waiting for someone you love who is late. But this was not just one person Mitchell was waiting for. This was everyone and every thing that he loved. He began to wonder whether there were some strange time-warp effects on the dark side of the moon, and whether he and the others were trapped in an eternal night. Mitchell reported that the minutes began to feel like days; the time behind the moon was becoming eternity.

the power of spiritual intelligence

After what seemed like aeons, they came out the other side.

And there, at last, was the Earth!

But the Earth was not as Mitchell had imagined. In his mind it had been the giant planet on which the universe of his home and family existed. What he saw now was a tiny blue planet floating in the vast inky blackness of space. Surrounding it was a fragile, wafer-thin covering of white – our entire atmosphere. Mitchell felt that he could literally reach out with his hand and flick the Earth, like a tiny pearl, into oblivion.

That moment, and that sudden realization of the fragility of our local home in the vastness of our big home, caused a paradigm shift in Edgar Mitchell. When he returned to Earth he felt far more compassion and concern for his fellow living beings, and decided to devote the rest of his life to helping protect this delicate, unique and beautiful planet.

A love of and respect for Nature is very characteristic of the Spiritually Intelligent. The tribal peoples we so often admire for their Spiritual Intelligence, such as the Native Americans and the Aborigines of Australia, are renowned for their deep concern for the conservation of the environment, for their respect and love for animals and other living things, and for their reverence for and awe of the Universe. This springs from an affiliation to and with the earth, and a feeling of responsibility to act as its guardians.

Nurture Yourself in Nature

Spiritual inspirations often make themselves known through music and poetry, and musicians and poets often see nature as their muse.

Byron, in *Childe Harold's Pilgrimage* wrote:

'There is a pleasure in the pathless woods,
There is a rapture on the lonely shore.
There is society, where none intrudes,
By the deep Sea, and music in its roar ...'

Similarly the visionary poet, artist and mystic William Blake wrote:

'When thou seeest an eagle, thou seeest a portion of Genius.
Lift up thy head!'

And when writing of an ideal approach toward the Universe, Blake penned the immortal lines:

'To see a World in a Grain of Sand
And a Heaven in a Wild Flower
Hold Infinity in the palm of your hand
And Eternity in an hour.'

Beethoven, Mozart and many other great musicians used Nature as their inspiration, incorporating into their music the songs of birds, the sounds of wind and water, the calls of animals and the sounds created by peasants and farmers going about their business. The entire four movements of Beethoven's Symphony no. 6 (Pastorale) were based on a walk in the countryside!

Nature has a way of rewarding those who investigate her, by enhancing their insights into all things, and thus raising their Spiritual Intelligence. One such example of someone who has been increasingly awed by the beauty and complexity of Nature is the British broadcaster Sir David Attenborough, whose prize-winning series on animals, plants and the natural world have amazed and inspired millions of viewers across the planet. Perhaps none have been more captivated by the wonders of nature than Sir David himself.

If you think about the following, you will understand why he and others, such as Jane Goodall and Dian Fossey in their work with endangered apes and gorillas, have become so fascinated by the natural world.

- How did a plant learn to mimic the shape, colourings and scent of a female wasp in order to attract the male to mate with 'her' and thus pollinate the flowers?
- How did a giant seed evolve that requires a forest fire once every 50 years to burn off its casing and allow it to reproduce?
- How does the Monarch Butterfly know the way from Europe to its precise nesting ground in Mexico?
- How does the salmon, after years swimming the oceans, know *exactly* where its original spawning ground is?

This reverence for life and living things is an important part of Spiritual

Intelligence; if you habitually swat flies, bugs and spiders, go to the bottom of the class!

brought to life by near-death experiences!

Many Spiritually Intelligent people report that it was often a near-death trauma that 'woke them up' from their spiritual sleep. One such experience certainly had me appreciating life more after it than before!

Teri and his Second Life

A good friend of mine, Teri, was a very fit and athletic man, a cyclist, rock-climber and caver. The end of his 'first life' came when climbing down the sheer face of a smuggler's cave. He grabbed a small outcrop of rock and it came away in his hand. His last conscious moments were spent realizing that he was falling backwards 180 feet, cracking his head on a rocky jut on the way down, and ending up in a bloody heap at the bottom with a smashed knee, broken leg, foot, arm, ribs, a punctured lung and a cracked skull.

Teri's 'second life' began in hospital when he regained consciousness and realized that he had been 'born again'. Everything appeared to him much brighter, more memorable and meaningful. Thirty years on Teri still reports that being given a 'second life' comprehensively changed his attitude to every day in that new life. Each day is a gift, and he spends each day enjoying every

---

moment of it. He is known as a wonderfully caring and compassionate man, with a gift for putting others at ease with his generosity and humour.

As he so succinctly puts it: 'Well, when you get a second chance at life, it does make you see things differently and appreciate what you've got a lot more, doesn't it?'

Tony and the 'Floating Balloon'

On holiday in the Caribbean, I was taking an early-morning swim in an exquisitely beautiful bay with crystal-clear blue water, mirror flat from the calm of the night before. Not particularly paying attention to where I was going, I ended up doing a long and leisurely series of back-strokes. When I stopped to turn around, I saw what looked like a blown-up balloon on the surface of the water, and without thinking (always dangerous!) I swam towards it. I noticed that the colour of the water underneath it appeared to be not so much blue as a beautiful lavender. Suddenly my brain recognized the danger signs, and screamed at me:

'*Portuguese Man-of-War!*'

Terrified, I swung about in the water – too late. The beautiful purple tendrils wrapped themselves around my waist and legs and sent me rocketing out of the water in pain. It felt as if I had been wrapped in barbed wire through which giant electric shocks were being pulsed.

I suddenly remembered (and understood!) the many reports I'd heard of people who had died of such an experience. For the next 10 or 15 minutes I was like some Walt Disney cartoon character with my legs thrashing like an outboard motor in the effort to get back to shore! With every stroke I wondered whether the poison was going to kill me rapidly, or lock all my muscles into an immovable rigidity that would lead me to drown.

The fact that you are reading this book means that you know I made it! I spent a little time in hospital, and came out still shocked, having been taught a number of lessons by Mother Nature – among them that I need to be more observant and more alert to danger.

Most importantly, however, I had learnt, while facing the prospect of having no days left, to pay much more attention to appreciating and enjoying the 'gift' of every day that I had and would be given.

do you make a difference?

**'God sleeps in the rock,
dreams in the plant,
stirs in the animal,
and awakens in mankind.'**

(Sufi teaching)

Believing that they can make a difference is another hallmark of the Spiritually Intelligent.

Do you make a difference?

Of course you do! Everything you say, do or create affects the environment and the people around you, and it and they affect others, and so on for infinity and eternity. This cause and effect can be confirmed by Chaos Theory – according to which a butterfly beating its wings in the Amazon rainforest can cause sufficient air turbulence to eventually cause a typhoon in Java.

You and your soul are 'immortal' whether you wish them to be or not! The real choice you have is whether that 'immortality' affects the human race and the planet in a positive way; whether you wish to leave it to chance; or whether you wish to work to its disadvantage. The Spiritually Intelligent person obviously chooses the first of these options!

Now that you are aware of your own magnificence, the vastness and the beauty of the universe in which you live, of the wonderful nature of Nature, and the fact that your spirit is immortal, you are ready for a good Spiritual Workout.

spiritual workout

1 Remind Yourself How Miraculous You Are

Remind yourself just what a magical work of design you really are. Make it a point to track down more information about the extraordinary capabilities of your human body and brain. Go to your local library or bookstore and dig out some of the popular science books around at the moment – on everything from brains to genes! Alternatively, watch some of the popular science programmes on TV. Constantly apply this knowledge to your own self-awareness and to the development of your self-confidence.

2 Remember that Everyone is Miraculous

Apply your new-found knowledge of your own magnificence to everyone around you – your friends, family, children, colleagues, people you meet on the street, and yes (this is a book on *Spiritual* Intelligence!), even your enemies. Once you begin to realize that everyone is as unique a person as you are, you will find yourself looking at people in a new light: each one with the spark of divinity in them. Decide what you can do to appreciate, help and learn from them more.

3 Learn from Your Life's Events

Look back over your life and its major events, traumas, pains and failures. Realize that every one of these is something that is strengthening your Spirit. Do everything you can to help that experience accelerate your growing strength – seek out the positive aspects, the silver linings, and all the possible lessons you can learn.

4 Learn to Appreciate the Natural World

Spend some time appreciating the multi-sensory beauty that surrounds you. Go for walks in the countryside as often as you can, or in parkland or some beautiful botanical garden (if you are lucky enough to live near one). Drink in the fresh air, the different scents and sounds, and the peace. Try doing this alone, as well as with your family or friends.

5 Play the 'Uniqueness Game'

Consider how many thoughts you have had in your life so far. Now think how many other people could have thought *exactly* the same thought, at *exactly* the same time, in *exactly* the same place?

You are unique amongst all the human beings who have ever lived, who do live and who will ever live. You are alone in this vast universe. But by being alone, you become like the six billion other human beings on the planet who are also alone. You are *together* in being *alone*! Think about it, and marvel at your simultaneous individuality and community.

6 Star Gaze!

Look up at the stars at night and try and get to know the different constellations – better still, invest in a basic telescope and really begin to explore the heavens. It is an amazing fact, but the entire universe you are seeing, you are recreating in your head! Just think – the tiny, microcosmic *you* can take in, hold and recreate the *universe*!

7 Ask Yourself Questions

Asking yourself questions such as:

- Does the universe end? If so, how and where? And if not, how not?
- Could our entire universe be simply an atom in a much bigger universe?

- Is there a unifying force that makes all this work? And if so, what is it?

Let your imagination roam – better still, ask your friends and colleagues too, and see what sort of creative, imaginative answers you can come up with. Read books by cosmologists and scientists who are exploring the frontiers of knowledge about the universe and its inhabitants.

8 The Weather

Whenever you are encouraged by the media, friends or your own personal thoughts to moan about the weather, think of the other options!

- **Mercury:** 1000 degrees centigrade on its sunny side, airless, more radiated than a microwave, and near absolute zero centigrade on its dark side!
- **Venus:** 450 degrees centigrade average temperature, battered by over 400-mile-an-hour sulphuric acid winds, with never any sight of the night-time sky.
- **Mars:** often minus 100 degrees centigrade. Hardly any atmosphere and no oxygen. Sun just visible as a big star. Inhospitable to life.
- **Jupiter, Uranus and Neptune:** all giant planets with gravity so strong you would be crushed the minute you set foot on them, which you couldn't do anyway, as their surfaces are liquid gasses. Average winds of 1000 miles per hour that never cease. No oxygen.

- **Pluto:** a tiny, airless planet less than the size of our moon with no sunlight, no atmosphere and a temperature near absolute zero.

In contrast, **Planet Earth:** Paradise! So delicately balanced to guarantee your survival that changes of less than 1 per cent in the 'formula' that created it would have made it inhospitable to life and therefore to you.

Therefore *enjoy* the weather – it's all good! Enjoy every variation from heatwave to freezing to wind to rain to frost to mist to snow. It is these very variations that allow the system to survive, grow and to support you.

9 Take Time-outs

Whenever you find yourself rushing about 'fire-fighting' one mini crisis after another, pause for a moment. Use these breaks as a spiritual tool to give your life context and meaning. These 'thought pauses' will help to give you a mechanism for coping, providing a constant pool of calm that will act to damp down all the little fires.

Again in times of hurry and stress, make a conscious effort to remember all the good 'spiritual stuff' that is happening 'out there': people striving for goals; parents trying to help and educate their children; charities attempting to do good; musicians playing and singing; artists drawing and painting; writers writing; and people dreaming of and working towards a better world. Remember that you are part of this 'Big Picture' – that you are a member of a planet-wide team, and must have the courage to continue with your own plans and ideals.

spirit boosters

As mentioned in the Introduction, these Spirit Boosters are for you to repeat to yourself silently, to say or sing aloud, or to write and hang up where you can see them regularly. Like all affirmations, when you continue to repeat them regularly, you *will* increase the likelihood that they become true.

- I am a miraculous work of art and design, and I continually explore and develop my potential.
- Every day I have more care for other living beings.
- I am both unique and the same as all other human beings. I explore these senses of individuality and community.
- Everything I say, do and create has incalculable, everlasting effects. I endeavour to make these effects beneficial for myself and for others.
- I live on a paradise of a planet. I am thankful for the opportunity it gives me to live; grateful for the bounteous gifts it offers me; and am committed to caring for it and looking after it.

mind-maps®

An interesting mental exercise to supplement this Spirit Booster is to envision that you are an astronaut stranded in space (much as Edgar Mitchell thought he might be). Take a large sheet of paper and note down all the gifts that Earth offers and about which you would be dreaming of returning to if you *were* stranded in space, or trapped on one of the other beautiful but inhospitable-to-life planets of our solar system.

Alternatively, you could Mind-Map® your thoughts. Mind-Maps® are fun and very easy to create, and they are wonderful ways to organize and remember your notes and thoughts, because they work with the brain's natural creativity, rather than against it!

To start your Mind-Map®, begin in the centre of a blank piece of paper and draw an image of your central idea (in this case planet Earth). From that central image, radiate off colourful, curved lines, rather like tree branches, each containing a *one-word* concept that springs to mind when you think about being stranded in space, dreaming of Earth. Then, take each one of the first level of concepts, and jot down what springs to mind when you consider those words, and so on to the next levels!

Make your Mind-Map® as colourful and as pictorially inventive as you can – your brain doesn't think in a linear fashion, but uses colour and images instead. Take a look at the examples in the plates in this book to see how beautiful and fun Mind-Maps® can be.

exploring your values

chapter two

**'Be ye lamps unto yourselves;
rely on yourselves;
do not rely on any external help!
Hold fast to the Truth as a lamp!'**

(Buddha)

Values are our codes of internal conduct; the principles upon which we run our lives and make our decisions. As children our first values are given to us by our parents, and these are supplemented later by values added from our peers, teachers, religious beliefs and our wider community. From these we select, consciously or unconsciously, the principles that we decide will rule our behaviour and our lives.

Values are the morals and standards of behaviour we set for ourselves, and they most commonly include such universal concepts as truthfulness, honesty, fairness, justice, honour, etc. Such standards of behaviour are essential for both personal and social survival – without them chaos and anarchy would erupt, and civilization would be extinguished in very short order!

When you have completed this chapter you will have had the opportunity to consider the main values selected by civilizations and the great spiritual thinkers throughout the ages. From these you will be able to select those Spiritual Intelligence principles that you feel will most helpfully guide your own life and behaviour, and provide a solid and comforting foundation for all your moral, ethical and other decision-making.

'The challenge to each human is creation.
Will you create with reverence,
Or with neglect?'

(Gary Zukav)

good news from the brain front!

Your Thoughts are Real

Research has shown that your thoughts are not simply 'airy fairy' things that exist in some never-never land. Thoughts are very real electro-magnetic, bio-chemical signals that carry messages across the network of your brain cells – rather like a chain of hilltop warning beacons being lit, one after the other, across the country.

What's more, like forging a path through a forest, each time a particular electro-magnetic, bio-chemical signal (a thought) goes along a particular route, its reception becomes easier and easier (as the path becomes more and more established), and the probability that that thought will have its desired effect becomes more and more certain.

Negative thinking results in greater negativity, whereas positive thinking improves health, prospects, creativity and more. It is exactly the same principle with values. If your values are counter-productive to your own and others' health and well-being, you will increase the probability that your own life and theirs will be unsatisfactory. If your values are positive they will do both yourself and others good.

The repetition of actions surrounding your values rapidly become habits, and these habits are the basis for much of your character and its expression.

'The thought manifests as the word;
The word manifests as the deed;
The deed develops into habit;
And habit hardens into character.
So watch the thought and its ways with care.
And let it spring from love
Born out of concern for all beings.'

(Buddha)

Now you are aware of the power of thought, it means that you can regain control of your own life, and escape from false feelings of being dogged by bad luck, etc. *You* can help create your own bad or good fortune, and so *you* can take responsibility for yourself and your actions.

Synergy

Research has also confirmed that your brain is synergetic, meaning that its thinking processes naturally multiply and expand, much as they do when you are daydreaming or fantasizing.

Therefore, if you fill your head with good and positive values, these will tend to multiply internally. This internal multiplication will express itself in your actions, and will begin to affect others around you. As *their* brains are also synergetic, you will have been responsible for creating a domino effect in both yourself and others that magnifies the good. You will become, much like my own Angel of Mercy, an ambassador for positive values and Spiritual Intelligence.

**'Whoever intercedes
with intervention for good
partakes thereby of it;
and whoever intercedes
with intervention for ill
shares thereby in it.'**

(Muhammad)

Truth and Honesty – Your Brain's Natural State

One of the most cheering pieces of news to come from the Brain Front laboratories is that we as human beings are naturally honest, and naturally interested in the truth. Our brains are in fact *truth-seeking mechanisms*!

Why should this be?

The answer is simple: we need to know the truth in order to survive.

For example, if you do not know the truth of what happens when a two-ton lorry travelling at 40 miles an hour comes into contact with a relatively static human form, that may well be the last realization of your life!

We *need* to know the truth about every cause and effect; we need to know what is going on around us, both within and beyond the immediate grasp of our senses; we *need* to know Truth.

That is why virtually all the great artists and scientists – Newton, Einstein, da Vinci, Cezanne, Dali, Picasso, etc. – all said they were searching for it.

It is also why young children are so insistent on *absolute* adherence to Truth and Honesty, and are devastated when their parents veer from what they have promised or said. The angry accusation 'but that's not *fair*, you *said* ...' is an expression of anger; more importantly, it is an expression of *fear*.

Fear of what?

Fear of not being able to Trust what someone else has purported to be the Truth. Fear of the incredible and terrifying uncertainty produced by contradictory information. Fear, in other words, for survival. For if the data a child's brain is given is inaccurate or contradictory, and if the child acts on such information, he or she is fully aware of the fact that his or her chances of survival are lessened. In just the same way, our cave-dwelling ancestors had to be able to Trust one another: if one man said that a particular cave was a great place to live, the others had to trust he wasn't lying and that the cave was not in fact already the home of a large, fierce, unfriendly bear!

When you search for the Truth, which is your natural tendency and your natural right, you are helping both yourself and others to survive. Conversely, when you are dishonest with yourself and others, you are lessening your and their chances of survival. You are increasing the probability that both you and they will act on false information, and therefore compound errors in behaviour and action that could put your best interests at risk.

It is this philosophical question – 'Is it better to act dishonestly for short-term good or honestly for possible short-term disadvantage and long-term gain?' – that has been the subject of much debate down the ages.

You, as well as the great geniuses of all time, and the Universe, suggest that the long-term pursuit of Truth is the better option!

It is now time for your Spiritual Workout, during which you will be able to consider a giant smorgasbord of values from which you can select the ones that you wish to guide you through the rest of your life.

spiritual workout

1 Code of Conduct

In this time of rapidly changing morals, pressures to conform and growing selfishness, having your own set code of personal conduct or firmly established values can make your life much easier. If you have a few strong values, and a clear line of behaviour beyond which you will not go, the easier it is to deal with dilemmas and situations as they arise.

2 Spiritual Values

Among the most commonly mentioned Spiritual Values are:

Truth	Honesty	Courage	Simplicity
Compassion	Co-operation	Freedom	Peace
Love	Understanding	Charity	Responsibility
Tolerance	Integrity	Trust	Purity
Unity	Gratitude	Humour	Persistence
Patience	Justice	Equality	Harmony

No doubt you can think of a few more as well.

From these select your 'Top 7' which you can use as the beacons for your own behaviour and as the principles upon which to base your moral, ethical and spiritual life.

(It is advisable to include Truth and/or Honesty among them, as these form a good foundation from which all the others can spring.)

3 Mind-Map® Your Values

When you have selected your Top 7 life-values, make a Mind-Map®
based on them (as you did in Chapter 1, see page 21). Create an image
that summarizes your own code of conduct, and have each of your
seven main ethical values emanate from the centre as main branches.
From each branch add words that you associate with that particular
idea, underlining or putting in boxes those that you consider to be the
most important.

4 Live Your Values

For each of your Top 7 values, think exactly how you can put them into
practice – list specific activities that you can do to make sure you live
by your values.

For example, if one of your top values is Charity, be generous with
your time and money – help out with your local bring-and-buy sale, or
at least donate some unwanted possessions. Also, try to think the best
of other people – even (perhaps especially) when they are thoughtless
or rude, or when you find them very, *very* irritating.

If Integrity is important to you, make sure that you do what you
say you will do: if a colleague at work tells you something in confidence,
don't go spreading it around the rest of the office; if you regard
yourself as an honest person, hand the lost wallet you find on the
pavement in to the local police – don't just pocket the money thinking
'Finders, Keepers!'

Living by your own internal values, you will avoid all the stress and
hassle that uneasy consciences and morally dubious actions generate,

and will be using your Spiritual Intelligence to your own best advantage
and to the benefit of the greater good!

5 Discuss Your Values

By discussing your values with your family, friends and colleagues
you will gain a deeper understanding of yourself, a refining of what you
have thought, and a deeper understanding of those with whom you
discuss your values.

Talking your values over will help you to ensure that they really *are*
important to you.

**'I can see that the great part of the miseries of mankind are brought upon them
by false estimates they have made of the value of things.'**

(Benjamin Franklin)

6 Trust Yourself

Rely on and have confidence in yourself. Anyone can give values to
you, but for them really to work, they have to be internalized; they have
to become part of you. When you make this decision, when your moral
principles and good values grow within you of their own accord, they
become like supple steel muscles that protect you against all attacks
and give you unbounded strength and power.

'Think good, do good, speak the truth.'

(Zoroaster)

7 Remember – Your Actions Matter

Continually remind yourself that your actions *do* have an effect, no matter what those actions are. In our speeded-up society we tend to wish for immediate cause and effect; for an immediate result to what we do. But think again. How often you have done something good, only for its result to manifest itself *years* later. My Angel of Mercy had no idea that her acts of kindness, compassion and love would one day result in a book which featured her and was being read by you!

8 Get Rid of Any 'Spiritual Blocks'

Review your life and see if there are any situations that are 'bugging you' because you are holding back from telling the truth you want to tell, or you are conscious of some action you've done in the past of which you are ashamed. If there are any such situations, find ways of 'righting any wrongs' – be honest and tell the truth you want to, and try to put right past wrong actions.

9 Role Models

Select seven role models from history and/or the present, whom you consider to be ideal role models for the pursuit of Truth and for virtuous/moral/ethical behaviour. Whenever you are in a moral dilemma, use them as an internal 'Mastermind Group' of advisors. 'Ask' each one in turn what they would do in your situation. You'll be surprised and pleased with the results! You will also be comforted and strengthened by the knowledge that you have such powerful new friends and allies.

spirit boosters

- I hold Truth and Honesty to be beacons for my life. I am increasingly honest with myself and others, and take pleasure in this.
- I am an ethical and moral human being. I use my principles to enhance my own life and the lives of those around me.
- I am reliable and dependable. My word is my bond.
- I am a just person. I am increasingly fair in all my dealings.
- I am an honourable person, and am directing my behaviour and life towards that which I feel to be good.

Steve Redgrave - Focus & dedicatio

Mother Teresa. - Compassion.

Jonothan Edwards - Spiritual Intell.

Sebesha Cee -

Tom Gordan.

Janet Jardine - Thoughtful / intelled.

Ursule. - calm.

chapter three

'Where there is no vision, the people perish.'

(Proverbs 29: 18)

Vision, in the Purpose-of-Your-Life sense, is defined as the ability to think about or plan the future with imagination and wisdom, incorporating a mental image of what that future could and will be like.

As a visionary-in-the-making you are going to think about your own future with imagination, wisdom and a little help from some of the great thinkers of all time!

Your life vision, plan or purpose is the goal to which you aspire and is the 'Guiding Light' of your life. If your goal is Spiritual, it needs to apply to you – and beyond.

The following reflection by Viktor Frankl epitomizes this:

> 'We who lived in the concentration camps can remember the men who walked through the huts comforting others, giving away their last piece of bread. They may have been few in number, but they offer sufficient proof that everything can be taken away from a man but one thing: The last of his freedoms – to choose one's attitude in any given set of circumstances, to choose one's own way.'

It is the lack of the 'beyond' in many people's goals that can lead apparently happy, well-off and successful people to come to realize that despite all their material, worldly success and affluence, their lives actually feel very empty and meaningless. This feeling of 'there must be more to life than this ...' is leading more and more people to reassess, re-evaluate and radically change their lives.

These people are developing their Spiritual Intelligence.

As you will be increasingly aware, the greater your Life-goal, the greater will be your probable impact on those around you and on history. The goals of the great spiritual leaders – Moses, Lao Tzu, Confucius, Jesus, Buddha, Muhammad – were infinite and eternal. Their works and influence today are greater than when they were alive.

In this chapter you will learn the 'Vision Formula' I have developed to help athletes, students and anyone with a brain who wants to learn to use it, to achieve success. This formula will help to give you added meaning and direction to your life – boosting your confidence, increasing your interest in the world around you, enabling you to make friends more easily, and giving you surprising new reserves of strength, stamina and power.

the spiritual vision formula

The great genius Johann Wolfgang von Goethe, writer, artist, athlete, politician and visionary, inspired a wonderful quote about vision and purpose in life, which is well worth contemplating as you decide on your own spiritual goal:

'Until one is committed there is hesitancy, a chance to draw back ... There is one elementary truth – the ignorance of which kills countless ideas and splendid plans. This is, that the moment one definitely commits oneself, then Providence moves too. All sorts of things occur to help one, that would never otherwise have occurred. A whole stream of events issues from the decision, raising in one's favour all manner of unforeseen incidents and material assistance, which no man could have dreamed would have come his way. Whatever you can do or dream you can, begin it. Boldness has genius, power and magic in it, begin it now.'

What this means is that when you refine your vision, which you are about to do, this new purpose will *immediately* begin to affect your behaviour and action, and will shift your daily focus, giving your life a direction that will attract to you new people, new ideas and new forms of energy.

The formula for creating an effective life-purpose consists of three elements:

1 It must be personally directed by you (you therefore have to say 'I').
2 It must commit you to action (you can't say 'wish', 'hope' or 'might').
3 It must be positive.

Wonderful examples of such goals include that of Isaac Newton, which was simply

'I am searching for the Truth.'

In contrast, an example of an *in*effective goal would be something like, 'I am going to help make the world less evil.' This concentrates on the negative, creating unnecessary unpleasantness and stress.

It is now time for a Spiritual Workout!

spiritual workout

1 Decide on Your Life Goal

Commitment is paramount. It is essential for you to begin to commit
now. Your vision does not have to be final or irrevocable. It *is* important
that you start to dedicate yourself to a goal that you know will benefit
yourself and others. As time progresses and your experience grows,
you will be able to adjust this goal as you see fit.

Don't feel afraid to copy, either. If you want to start with Isaac
Newton's or with any others from *The Power of Spiritual Intelligence*,
then borrow theirs!

Once you have selected your vision and purpose and are committed
to it, you need to write it out, and repeat it to yourself, ideally at least
five times a day. Every repetition will make your commitment to your
vision stronger, and will increase the probability of success.

2 Own Your Vision

Once you have your vision in place, remember that it is *your* vision
and yours alone. It is like a special gift that the universe has given you
– an ultimate pep-pill or vitamin tablet, which gives you incredible
energy and does you only good.

The following poem by William Henley, quoted by Martin Booth
in his *Industry of Souls* will serve as a constant and ideal reminder for
you:

> 'It matters not how strait the gate,
> How charged with punishments the scroll,
> I am the master of my fate:
> I am the captain of my soul.'

3 Help Others

'One truth stands firm. All that happens in world history rests on something spiritual. If the spiritual is strong, it creates world history. If it is weak, it suffers world history.'

(Albert Schweitzer)

Make a habit of contributing to others and to society. Do this with a positive attitude.

For example, if you see rubbish in the street, don't curse those who are so spiritually and environmentally unaware that they thoughtlessly dumped it there. Don't leave it there for others to have the same unpleasant experience as you – pick it up!

Help others, too, to develop the same spiritual awareness as yourself, encouraging *them* to work towards *their* life vision. The best help is by example, as actions always speak louder than words!

4 Responsibility # 1 – Make the World a Better Place

Whatever your Vision is, it will incorporate a sense of responsibility. Resolve that your path through life will be marked by events and actions, both large and small, that leave the world a better place for your passing through. These actions do not all have to be major, world-changing events (abolishing hunger and world debt at a stroke, for example). Small actions are just as important, and all add to the sum of human happiness: give up your seat (graciously!) on the train or bus for someone less able to stand; if you rent a cottage or apartment for a holiday, make sure you leave it clean and tidy, and think about placing some fresh flowers there for the next occupants; if you can, plant a tree or seedling in your garden, or donate one to your local park – you won't see the benefit of your actions, but your grandchildren will.

5 Responsibility # 2 – Make Yourself a Better Place!

'Responsibility is the price of greatness.'

(Winston Churchill)

Remember, for your Vision to be realized, you need to be 'fighting fit'. The longer you're around, the more you can contribute – so watch your diet, and make sure that you have a regular 'meal' of exercise (at least three times a week), in which you give your heart and muscles a good workout.

6 Be Inspired by Others

Whenever you get the opportunity, read about or discuss the great figures in history, especially the spiritual ones. Find out what their visions were and how they fought to make them come true. Learn every lesson you can, and then try to apply them!

7 Check Your 'Self Talk'

'Self Talk' refers to those constant little conversations that go on in your head between you and you! In many cases these tend to be negative, especially in learning or skill-based situations. Such phrases as 'I'll never be able to do this', 'I'm stupid', 'Damn it, what *is* the point?' 'I'm worse than everybody else', 'I don't have the talent for this', 'I give up!' are common.

Your Life Vision needs to be positive, *and so does your 'Self Talk'*. If it is negative, it eats away at your success; if it is positive it will support your growing success.

8 Be on the Look Out for Vision-supporting Statements

Constantly scan the media for statements and lessons that support and reinforce your Vision. In a recent TV interview, the golfing phenomenon Tiger Woods attributed his meteoric rise in the world of golf to one of his prime personal goals – learning from every experience: '*At the end of every tournament, to review every stroke and every hole, seeing what I can learn from the experience.*'

Be like Tiger.

Your Brain is born to learn, so take every opportunity, in everything you do, to review and to enhance the power of your Spiritual Intelligence, by incorporating into your subsequent activities the lessons you have learned.

'No man that does not see visions will ever realise any high hope or undertake any high enterprise.'

(Woodrow Wilson)

9 Remind Yourself that Your Life is a Gift

Always remember that your life is a precious gift – live it fully and well!

spirit boosters

- When my life is done I will have left a trail of positive and good actions on the earth.
- Every day, in every way, my Spiritual Intelligence is getting better and better.
- I am a positive individual, spreading my positive energy to others.
- I am responsible for the welfare of myself and others, and enthusiastically and actively accept that responsibility.
- My life is the most magnificent of gifts. I am using that gift to give and contribute to the planet that gave birth to me.

compassion –

understanding yourself and others

chapter four

'No man is an Island, entire of it self; every man is a piece of Continent, a part of the main; if a clod be washed away by the sea, Europe is the less, as well as if a promontory were, as well as if a manor of thy friends, or of thine own were; any man's death diminishes me, because I am involved in Mankind;

And therefore never send to know for whom the bell tolls; it tolls for thee.'

(John Donne)

Compassion is expressing sympathy and concern for others in thought and action. It is a reaching out to others in a spirit of love and respect. A Spiritually Intelligent and compassionate person will have a sense of commitment to others, and will take responsibility for helping them.

The good news (and for some, the most difficult task) is that the first person you have to be compassionate towards is *yourself*! You

need to respect yourself, care for yourself, be committed to yourself, and take responsibility for helping yourself to become all that you can be.

'The core issue in uniting the dualistic energies of our relationships is to learn how to Honour One Another. So much of the way we respond to the external challenges is determined by how we respond to ourselves. In addition to all the relationships we have with people, we must also form a healthy and loving relationship with ourselves ...'

(Caroline Myss)

It is only when you have compassion for yourself, when you have cultivated and enhanced it, that you can extend that compassion to include and embrace others.

The Dalai Lama has said that you could, in one sense, define Compassion as:

'The feeling of unbearableness at the sight of other peoples' suffering, other sentient beings' suffering. In order to generate that feeling one must first have an appreciation of the seriousness or intensity of another's suffering. The more fully one understands suffering, and the various kinds of suffering that we are subject to, the deeper will be one's level of compassion.'

A Spiritually Intelligent person will therefore be far more *understanding* of people, and the causes and significance of actions and reactions in others. As a result the person who has developed the power of compassion will be more forgiving, more tolerant, and will allow others to exist without unnecessarily interfering in their lives. As Eleanor Roosevelt said, *'Understanding is a two-way street.'*

Think of compassion as the 'art of being happy'. It is the art of transforming pain and suffering into happiness and joy.

What better goal could you have in life?

When you learn this art you will, naturally, become more happy and joyful! In the process you will also become more open-minded, and establish deeper friendships, based on mutual understanding and respect. By understanding your and others' suffering, you will gain deeper insights into yourself and the human condition. In short, your life will gather depth, meaning, purpose and joy.

compassionate tales...

In order to demonstrate the nature of compassion and its practice, I offer you the following compassionate tales.

The Tibetan Monk's Tale

The Dalai Lama tells the story of a senior monk at the Namgyal Monastery. He was arrested by the occupying Chinese forces and held as a political prisoner in forced labour camps for 20 years,

---

where he faced severe beatings and torture, continuing and remorseless pain, difficulty and suffering.

The young Dalai Lama once asked his friend what had been the most difficult situation he had faced when he was in prison.

The answer was not anything to do with either his physical and mental suffering, nor the sufferings of the other prisoners, a number of whom were killed.

The monk said that he felt the greatest danger he had ever faced was that of losing compassion for his Chinese captors!

Muhammad Ali and the Tramp

When he was at the height of his fame and power, feted around the world, Ali was walking through the poor district of Harlem, New York, followed (as usual) by a crowd of reporters. As he walked down one of the rubbish-filled streets, he noticed a dishevelled tramp half lying in the gutter.

Waving the reporters and cameras away, Ali crouched down and spent some time just talking with the man. After Ali had said goodbye and left, one reporter asked the tramp what he thought of 'The Greatest'.

'He *is* the Greatest' said the tramp.

'Why do you think that?' asked the reporter.

The tramp replied that Ali had asked him how he came to be in the gutter. He reported that he had told Ali the sad story of his life, and was overcome with tears as he told it.

He then gave the reason why he thought Ali was the greatest. The tramp said: 'I cried at him. *And he cried back at me.*'

The Two Presidents' Story

When reporting on the highlights of his Presidency, Bill Clinton said that his meeting with Nelson Mandela stood out. At the time of the meeting, Clinton was in all kinds of difficulties: America was involved in several armed conflicts, impeachment proceedings against him were in full swing, and his self-confidence was severely dented.

Mandela made a point of approaching Clinton and offered to help, saying to Clinton that everyone makes mistakes, and it is not so much the *mistakes* that matter, as how one *deals* with the suffering such mistakes cause.

Clinton asked Mandela how he could possibly be so tranquil and serene, especially after all he had suffered in his nearly 30 years in jail. Surely, Clinton asked, Mandela must still feel angry and the need for revenge.

Mandela explained that if he were to abide by his own principles, then revenge was irrelevant.

Like the Tibetan monk, Mandela focused on the pain and suffering of those who had made him suffer; forgave them, and moved on – to apply his vast energies to world-changing projects in education and social development, rather than harbouring grievances and wasting those same energies on vengeful thoughts or actions.

Clinton reported that the conversation made him more understanding of himself; more understanding of others; more committed; more forgiving; and more compassionate.

It changed his life.

confirming the benefits of compassion

In a fascinating experiment to show the effects of Compassion on the body, Dr David McClelland, a psychologist at Harvard University, showed a group of students a film of one of the heroines of *The Power of Spiritual Intelligence* – Mother Teresa of Calcutta. The film showed Mother Teresa at work among Calcutta's poor, sick and destitute. The students watching reported that the film made them feel compassionate.

Shortly after they had been shown the film, Dr McClelland analysed the students' saliva and found an increase in the antibody that helps fight respiratory infections – immunoglobulin A. Their feelings of compassion on watching Mother Teresa's work had stimulated the students' bodies to produce increased amounts of this antibody.

In a further study on Compassion, Dr James House of the University of Michigan Research Center studied the effects of doing regular voluntary work with, for example, the sick and homeless.

The work the volunteers did obliged them to act towards others in a warm and compassionate manner over a period of months and years.

The results showed that doing such compassionate work increased overall vitality and dramatically increased the life-expectancy of the volunteers.

Compassion is a life-saver, not only for those to whom you show compassion – it is a life-saver for you as well!

Now that you know the nature of Compassion, and have proof of its effectiveness, as well as examples to back you up, you are ready for your next Spiritual Workout.

spiritual workout

1 Show Compassion

**'And when you are greeted
with a salutation,
offer a greeting nicer still,
or at least return it.'**

(Muhammad)

The ability to 'get on' with and to show compassion for your fellow humans is one of the elements that can make your life a joy or a battle. Every interaction that you have with any other human gives you the opportunity to leave them with a smile and for both of you to feel

---

uplifted. Alternatively you have the opportunity to stir up anger and resentment. Which will add more to the quality of your life and your physical and mental well-being? Just by considering this question you are already heading in the right spiritual direction.

2 Uniqueness Exercise

Below you will find the word 'Understanding' nestled in the centre of a heart. Off the heart radiate ten curved and organic branches – much

like the branches of a tree. The game is as follows: on the central branches, print the first 10 words that come into your head, whatever they are, when you think of the concept 'Understanding'.

When you are doing this exercise, let your mind flow free, and print whatever the first 10 words are that pop into your mind, no matter how 'far out' or ridiculous they might seem. When you have done this, read on.

When you have completed this exercise, compare your answers with others'. Here are the suggestions my editors came up with when they tried the exercise:

listening	knowledge
willingness to see the other's point of view	sense
tolerance	sympathy
openness of mind	feeling
attentiveness	compassion
empathy	empathy
sympathy	tolerance
truthfulness	forgiveness
open heartedness	enlightenment
observation	revelation

The amazing finding from this exercise, which I have done around the world for 30 years, is that there is very little commonality between people, and much more individuality than you might expect!

This means that you, as we first discovered in Chapter 2, are a preciously unique individual. It also means that so is everybody else! It *also* means that understanding things from other people's points of view is a much more complex, demanding, exciting and *rewarding* experience than we had previously thought.

Play this 'understanding' game with any other words or concepts you choose. It is especially interesting to play it with friends, family and colleagues around concepts which are important to you; concepts about which you disagree; or concepts that represent your common goals.

3 Have Compassion For Your Fellows

In all situations, try to consider why other people are acting the way that they are. Try always, especially in 'difficult' situations, to put yourself in the other person's place – there is an old Native American saying: 'Never judge a man until you have walked in his moccasins.' Treat others as you yourself would wish to be treated. This will help you to see things from the other person's perspective (which, to them, is always right!), and will help you show more understanding and compassion for them. In turn, this will make your life a lot easier, and your own spirit more calm and happy.

'Do unto others as you would have others do unto you.'

(Jesus of Nazareth)

4 Act for the Sake of the Act

Don't expect a certain response when you give appreciation or are compassionate towards someone. Give without thought of your own gain or benefit. Be open about how the person may or may not react, or you will just set both of you up for potential disappointment. You may never know the knock-on effect your action may have. Just know that you are happier for making the positive effort, and so, at some level, will they be. So smile, be happy and don't expect anything in return.

Actually, becoming detached from outcomes and expectations is one of the most difficult things to do, yet it is something that brings the greatest rewards. *And* detachment protects you from all the heartaches that often accompany those expectations.

5 Take Part in 'Random Acts of Kindness'

Joining the increasing number of people practising 'random acts of kindness', in a movement that is started in America and is growing elsewhere. These random acts are carried out anonymously, and can consist of something as simple as putting some money through the door of someone in need, or paying the road toll for the car behind.

6 Co-operate with Others!

Compassion is heightened by an attitude of co-operation. As such, look for ways in which you can work and interact with those around you. Reach out your hand quickly to assist wherever you can, and look for ways to work towards common goals with like-minded people. If

---

you do, it is likely that you will attain those goals faster, and the experience will be a richer one for being shared. When you work with others in this way, something good happens: your individual energies and enthusiasms don't simply add up to make the total. Each one of you multiplies the energy and strength of the others to create a whole which is greater than the sum of its parts.

7 Respect Your Fellow Humans

Each one of us is a miracle. It is commonly agreed that every person's life-story has all the potential to make a best-selling book, and that includes *you*! Think about it ... Rather than assuming things about someone, behave like a Compassionate Journalist, and ask them to let you know about the most interesting and meaningful aspects of their lives. Find out about their personal histories, their greatest moments in life, their fondest memories, their goals and their beliefs. Whatever a person's current circumstances, they carry with them – like Linus carries his blanket – all that they ever were and have done. Find out, admire, respect and enjoy!

8 Your 'Dark Side'

This is a challenging exercise - give it a go when you feel ready!

Consider that anyone in your life who is particularly difficult, mean, or downright nasty to you, is there *specifically* to help you advance in your own Compassionate Studies! Consider that they could be a mirror for your own hidden dark side, and learn from the experience. And remember:

'To err is human, to forgive, divine.'

(Alexander Pope)

9 The Blending Game

Imagine that the people close to you with whom you are fighting or loving are actually not separate people. They are a *part* of You; You are the combination of You and Them. In other words you are a larger self.

From this new perspective, see how this would change your perception, feelings and actions. It is particularly interesting to try this game in love/hate relationships; student/teacher relationships; boss/worker relationships, etc.

10 Trust Your Fellow Humans

It feels much nicer to trust people than not to trust them. Many people who have been let down or hurt, close *themselves* down emotionally, so as not to be hurt again. In so doing they stop living and feeling, and suffer much more in the long run. Give everyone you meet an 'A' grade, and as time goes on allow them either to add or subtract from their 'account'. At this point decide whether you wish to spend more or less time with them. Interestingly, if you expect the best from people and your relationships with them – from the person who serves you at a shop, to your best friend – you are more than likely to receive an 'A' from them in return!

'Trust men and they will be true to you; treat them greatly and they will show themselves great.'

(Ralph Waldo Emerson)

If you apply the Principles of Compassion learnt in this chapter, you can make significant changes to the many different communities of which you are part, especially the business community and wider political society, which are in much need of such help!

By becoming a compassionate business man or woman, you can help change the traditional business dynamic motivated by *profits*, which are generated by serving others, to that of *serving* others, which is made possible by profits. In politics this same dynamic applies, and is particularly relevant to changing the concept of *external* power being used to govern over others, to the dynamic that springs from *internal* compassion spread towards all other avenues of life.

spirit boosters

- I am growing more compassionate and understanding with every day.
- I am compassionate toward myself, focusing on the development of my Spiritual Intelligence.
- Because I am increasingly able to understand others, I am increasingly forgiving and tolerant.

- My deepening understanding of the miracle and complexity of others allows my mind to be increasingly open and flexible.
- I am always striving to do unto others as I would have them do unto me.

give and receive!

charity and gratitude

chapter five

> **'Be the living expression of … kindness; kindness in your face, kindness in your eyes, kindness in your smile, kindness in your warm greeting.'**

(Mother Teresa of Calcutta)

The twin Spiritual Graces of Charity and Gratitude are mirror images of each other. Charity is concerned with giving help for those in need, and being tolerant in judging that need. The word comes from the Latin *carus* which means 'valued' or 'loved'. With those who are dear or beloved, we are open-armed, open-hearted, magnanimous and altruistic. This is the spirit of Charity.

Gratitude is the opposite Grace. This is where you thankfully receive charity, understanding and selfless actions, and show your appreciation of the kindness that is offered to you.

Both Charity and Gratitude are born of the Compassion you explored in the previous chapter. The two actions can be considered as a kind of Spiritual breathing: Gratitude is where you breathe 'in' and receive life-giving energy; Charity is where you breathe 'out' and give back to the environment.

When you practise both Charity and Gratitude, you considerably expand the power of your Spiritual Intelligence. You learn to 'inhale' and 'exhale' in a rhythmical way, rather than to 'hold your breath' all the time. This will help you feel more relaxed, happy and 'at one' with the world.

In the same way as developing your Compassion, the rewards that accrue to you will include more friends, better health and more wealth – the unit of exchange in *this* currency is the smile! It will of course also benefit your wider community and world immeasurably.

'He is truly great who hath great charity'

(Thomas à Kempis)

The stories that follow are designed to amuse, inform, move and inspire you.

'trevor's campaign'

In 1983 a young boy by the name of Trevor Ferrell, saw a homeless
man living on the streets of Philadelphia. Later Trevor asked his
parents why the man slept on the cold street, and when he learned it
was because the man had no home or family to care for him, Trevor
asked his parents to drive him into the city so that he could give the
man his own pillow and yellow blanket. They did.

From this one act of compassion flowing from the uncluttered
heart of a 13-year-old, 'Trevor's Campaign' began. Every night since,
volunteers – adults and children – travel the streets of Philadelphia
distributing hot meals, blankets, clothing, caring and love – all
because of one young boy. Over the years, the Campaign has spread,
and now children and adults emulate Trevor's caring example in
towns and cities all over the world where the hungry homeless
dwell.

Trevor has spoken about his campaign in schools, assembly halls,
state houses, churches and town meetings. When Trevor was asked
if the Campaign's growth surprised him, he said, 'I never expected
there to be 1,100 volunteers, three vans and a house for the homeless.
All I wanted to do was help the homeless, one day at a time.'

His attitude is the same as that of Mother Teresa (with whom
Trevor worked for a while in India). She was asked why she
continued with her work, picking up the dying and rescuing children
from the streets, when the problem just continued, and that what
she did was only a 'drop in the ocean' compared to the many

thousands of the poor in need. She replied, *'Yes, it is true, my work is just a small drop in the ocean, but because of my one drop, the entire ocean is bigger.'*

juggling classes

In the classes that I give around the world on Learning How To Learn and Expanding Your Mind Power, one of the games we play is Learning How to Juggle, based on the juggling metaphor method developed by Mike Gelb. Juggling is a perfect learning opportunity and teaching tool, because it provides an immediate mirror for the way our brains approach any new learning task. It also gives lots of immediate feedback!

One sad aspect of these otherwise amusing classes concerns my students' reactions to my compliments on their progress. Whether they have just done their first three-ball-throw-and-catch, or whether they have just completed a complex and advanced trick, their replies to my encouragements and cries of 'Well done!' are always of the following order:

'No, No, No! I was trying for the next stage.'
'It's no good, I'm stuck here!'
'It *wasn't* that good.'
'I'll never really be any good.'
'It could have been better.'

And the common theme in all these responses?

Denial of self!

The amusing thing about this kind of reaction is that it doesn't matter how good the performance is, the individual *always* denies the excellence.

If someone were juggling with seven balls, one chainsaw and a live chicken, and I exclaimed 'Wow! That's incredible!', they would reply something like: 'Well, not really – I was trying for *eight* balls, *two* chainsaws, a chicken *and* a turkey!'

If we are criticized and punished for failure when we are young, and then told that we are arrogant if we are pleased with our successes, we become trained and accustomed to punishing ourselves almost no matter what we do. We continually reject and deny praise. — YES - me.

'There is as much greatness of mind in acknowledging a good deed, as in doing it.'

(Seneca)

In thinking we are being 'modest', we are at the same time, subtly and unwittingly, insulting the person who praises us. What the people whom I praised for their excellence in juggling were *actually* saying was: 'Tony, you're wrong! You're an idiot! How could you possibly think I was doing well when I know I wasn't.'

Pretty insulting behaviour towards someone trying to be meek, mild and humble!

The moral of this story is, of course, to accept thanks with gratitude, and in so doing receive the gifts that others are offering you, while recognizing and uplifting them in turn.

'Gratitude is heaven itself'

(William Blake)

the poor boy and the education of the world

In the middle of the 1800s, a 12-year-old Scottish boy by the name of Andrew Carnegie emigrated to Pittsburgh, Pennsylvania. From a poor family, he was obliged to start work at an early age, first in a cotton-spinning factory, then as a telegraph messenger boy, and next as a railway clerk, before going into steel manufacturing.

Young Carnegie had a remarkable faith in himself. He worked hard, and learned from his mistakes, and he rapidly rose to the top of his profession. Carnegie eventually built up the US Steel Corporation to become the biggest company in the world, and himself, arguably, the richest man.

Two things, for we who are in search of increased Spiritual Intelligence, stand out particularly about his life story.

First, Carnegie attributed the major part of his success to his study and application of the brain and its extraordinary powers for Creative and Spiritual Intelligences. He commented:

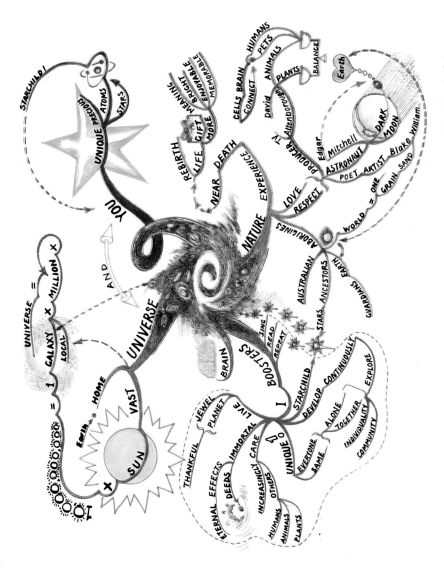

Summary Mind-Map® of Chapter 3

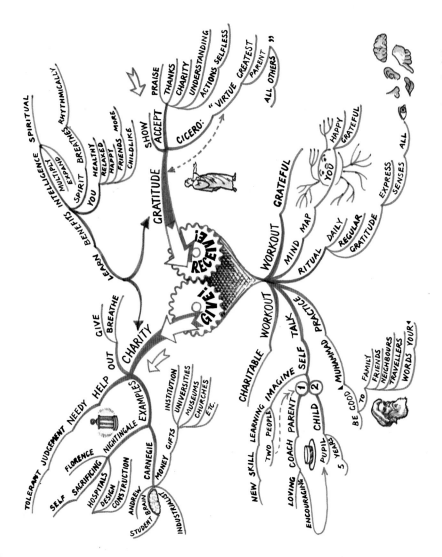

Summary Mind-Map® of Chapter 5

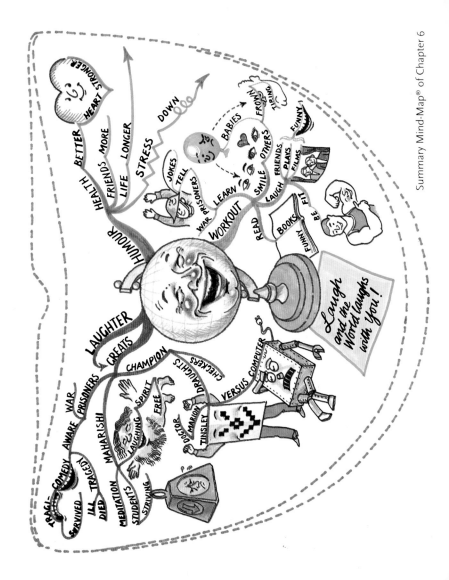

HEART STRONGER

HEALTH   BETTER   FRIENDS   MORE   LIFE   LONGER

STRESS   DOWN

JOKES   TELL

WAR   PRISONERS

BABIES   FROWN   TIRING

FUNNY

LEARN   OTHERS

WORKOUT   SMILE   FRIENDS   PLAYS   FILMS

LAUGH

READ   BE   FIT

BOOKS   FUNNY

HUMOUR

LAUGHTER

GREATS

CHAMPION

MAHARISHI   LAUGHING   SPIRIT   FREE

CHECKERS   DRAUGHTS

TRAGIC   COMEDY   WAR   PRISONERS   AWARE

ILL   TRAGEDY   DIED   SURVIVED

MEDITATION   STUDENTS   STRIVING

DOCTOR   MARION   TINSLEY   VERSUS   COMPUTER

Laugh and the World laughs with you!

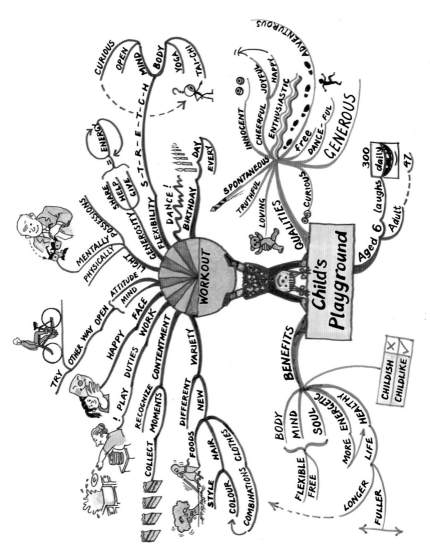

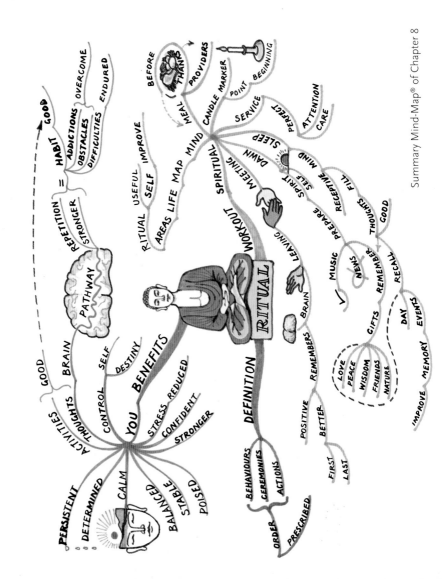

Summary Mind-Map® of Chapter 9

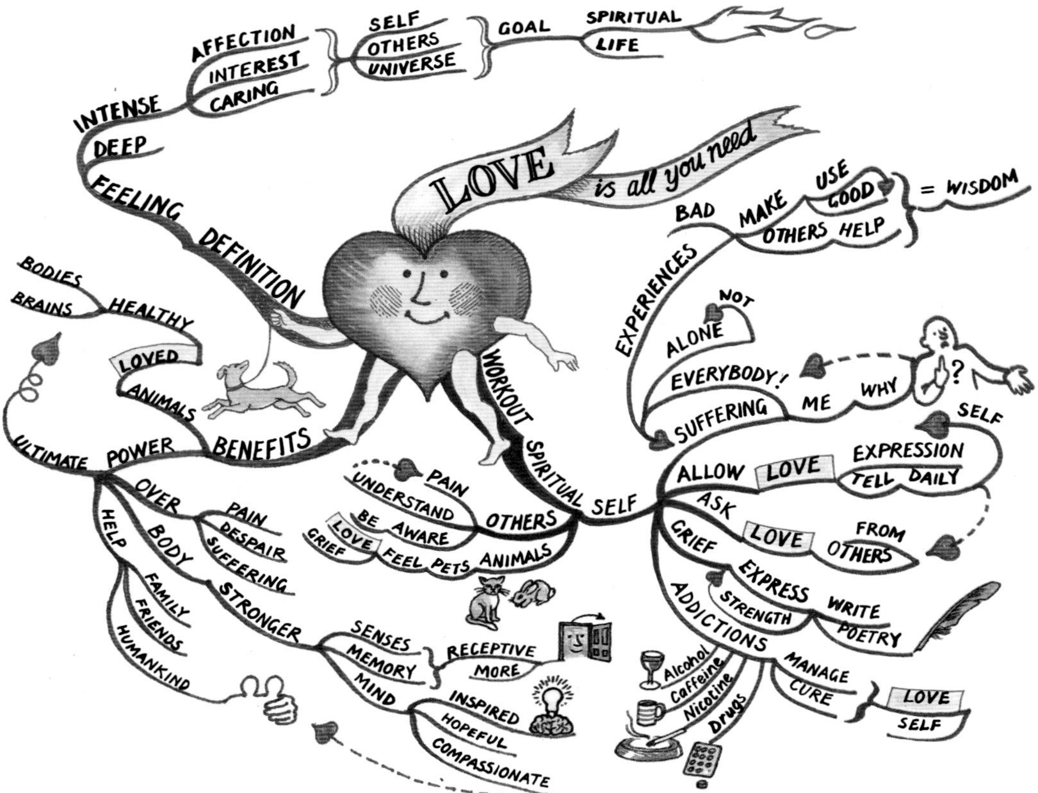

Summary Mind-Map® of Chapter 10

'Man, with all his boasted culture and education understands little or nothing of the intangible force (the greatest of all the intangibles!) of thought. He knows but little concerning the physical brain and its vast network or intricate machinery through which the power of thought is translated into its material equivalent; but he is now entering an age which will yield enlightenment on the subject.'

Carnegie recommended that *everyone everywhere* studied the brain and its Multiple Intelligences!

Second, when he retired in 1901, at the age of 66, Carnegie considered what to do with the vast riches that his hard work, intelligence and astuteness had enabled him to accumulate.

His decision?

To give it all away!

And to what purpose?

Learning and education.

In today's terms, Carnegie distributed over one hundred million dollars to global education, public libraries, Scottish and American universities, museums, art galleries and churches across Europe, and to his own Carnegie Institution, devoted to the cultural distribution of millions annually.

Andrew Carnegie transformed himself from the world's most successful industrialist into the world's most charitable educationalist. He gave away probably the largest fortune in history for the purpose of raising the educational standards and opportunities of his fellow humans.

Lighting the Jaws of Hell

Florence Nightingale is credited with making nursing the respected profession it has become, and who encouraged millions of others after her to follow her example.

She worked ceaselessly, with total commitment and absolute self-sacrifice to save lives and ease the pain and suffering of the appalling conditions of the Crimean War.

For the soldiers enduring wind, rain, snow, and semi-starvation, as well as terrible festering injuries in unsanitary conditions, Florence Nightingale was a beacon of hope, her charitable, practical actions giving faith and inspiration to those in despair.

After the war, Florence Nightingale continued to dedicate her energies to providing help and care for others. She revolutionized both nursing and hospitals – being responsible for the design of hospitals with well-lit, well-ventilated wards. London's famous St. Thomas's Hospital is just one example of her work.

It is the work of such great Spiritually Intelligent individuals as Andrew Carnegie and Florence Nightingale that laid the foundations for the modern focus on charitable institutions. At the beginning of the 21st century, there are thousands of organizations raising large sums each year for charitable causes across the world, all devoted to improving the human condition.

However, it is not just the 'big' acts of charity that count; the small, individual gifts of money, kindness or time (which is probably even more important in this increasingly busy world of ours) that we can all give matter just as much.

'...That best portion of a good man's life;
His little, nameless, unremembered acts
Of kindness and of love ...'

(William Wordsworth)

spiritual workout

You belong to a Charitable Race living on an increasingly Charitable Planet! As such a privileged resident of this planet, we are in a wonderful position to act charitably towards those many, many others who are in great need of our kindness. Therefore, it's best you keep your Charitable Self in shape.

1 Whom Should We Help?

Practice what the great spiritual leader Muhammad recommended:

'Be good to your parents
and relatives,
and to orphans and paupers,
and to neighbours close by
and neighbours remote,

---

and to the companion at your side,
and to the traveller,
and to your words.'

In fact, the giving of alms is one of the key practices of many of the world's great religions. Charitable giving is one of the five 'pillars' of the Islamic faith, and it is a central tenet of both Jewish and Christian practice, and also among Buddhists and Hindus.

'Charity sees the need, not the cause.'

(German Proverb)

2 'Self Talk'

Examine and reconsider your own Self Talk, as you did in Chapter 3, but this time give it a different twist. Consider it from the point of view of being *charitable to yourself,* and try the following Brain-game exercise.

Imagine that whenever you are learning something new, you are divided into two people: the first of the two is You-the-parent; the second is You-the-five-year-old-child.

The Parent-You takes the role of the ultimate coach; the Child-You the role of the learner. The Parent-You reacts to the Child-You as any loving and caring parent/coach would. You give words of encouragement, such as: 'Yes!'; 'That's it!'; 'Well done!'; 'You're

---

the power of spiritual intelligence

going to be a great juggler/footballer/guitar player, etc!'; 'That was an interesting mistake!'; 'Try again!'; 'Try again!'; 'Try again!'; 'You can do it!'; 'Well done!'

Being charitable to yourself in this way will give you tremendous encouragement and pleasure in learning. You will also find that the five-year-old you learns incredibly well, and will shower you with gratitude and affection!

3 Mind-Map®

Try to make a Mind-Map® of *everything* in your life for which you can be grateful. Don't just concentrate on the obvious things – friends, family, health – also think about the little things: the ability to feel the sun on your face or a gentle breeze on your skin, your sense of taste and smell, the way you listen to people and share with them, and so on.

'When we look deeply into the heart of a flower, we see clouds, sunshine, minerals, time, the earth, and everything else in the cosmos in it. Without clouds there could be no rain, and without rain there would be no flower.'

(Thich Nhat Hanh)

4 Be Appreciative of Small Things, and SAY So!

Make sure you give specific appreciation as you go through the day. Give appreciation to those you work and live with, and even see in passing. It is amazing how a quick compliment or 'thank-you' can make someone's day. Remember – all human beings have the same need for and appreciation of Appreciation and Compassion. Give appreciation to those people who serve and help you – to shop assistants, café waiters, rubbish collectors, street sweepers, office cleaners, bus drivers – and *especially* to those people who do all those 'horrible' jobs, and without whose work life would be much more unpleasant. Give appreciation to your friends and colleagues, *and* to your managers and bosses. Interestingly, people at the 'top of the tree', contrary to popular belief, often receive far less appreciation than people further down. Why? Because everyone assumes that everyone else is praising them!

5 Support Your Local Community

Support your local community by taking unwanted clothes to the charity shop, or the school fundraising event – or volunteer a few hours to help out. Or you could look after a neighbour's child for a few hours, or mentor a colleague at work – the possibilities for charitable action are infinite.

6 Support Your Wider Community

All too often natural disasters such as earthquakes, famines and floods are reported in the news, and our papers and TVs are filled with pictures of people in desperate plights. During such emergencies, try to give money, warm clothes or time to the relief effort. Lots of small actions, when added together, make a huge contribution to alleviating people's suffering.

7 Count Your Blessings

We can never be sure whether something will have a good or bad effect on our lives, so try to regard everything that happens as a 'blessing'.

There is an old Chinese story about a farmer whose horse strayed, and all his neighbours came round and commiserated with him, saying what bad luck it was; the farmer just replied, 'Is it?' The next day the horse returned, followed by another, and all the neighbours said what a stroke of fortune; again, the farmer just replied, 'Is it?' The following day the farmer's son tried to ride the new horse, but was thrown and his leg broken. Again, the neighbours all commiserated with the family's bad luck, and again the farmer replied, 'Is it?' The day after, the Imperial Army came to the village to conscript soldiers for the war. All the young men of the village were taken except the farmer's son, whose leg was broken.

spirit boosters

- I am a charitable person and love the act of giving.
- I am generous by nature, and am strengthening this part of my character.
- I am a nurturing and caring person, always willing to hold out a helping hand.
- I love receiving help, care and gifts from others, and do so openly and with enthusiasm. My receiving *allows* them to give. Their giving allows them to *receive*.
- I am a kindly and gentle person, always considering the needs of others.
- My creed is kindness.

give and receive! charity and gratitude

chapter six

'Laugh and the world laughs with you.'

(Ella Wheeler Wilcox)

It's true! Laugh and the world *will* laugh with you! A sense of humour is one of the major qualities of Spiritual Intelligence. Its benefits including less stress, a general improvement of health, and more (and more happy) friends. It leads to a happier, more cheerful and uplifting life.

Humour helps you to put things in perspective, and allows things to calm down. It has a wonderful way of diffusing tension and uniting people from all walks of life. It provides a common bond for humankind.

I experienced a dramatic example of the power of humour during the 1970s. A medium-sized student demonstration outside the American Embassy in London suddenly grew into a massed uprising of many thousands of people, who crammed into the small square in front of the Embassy.

I had been unwittingly strolling through the square, and suddenly found myself trapped near the front of the line, where police on horses were holding the increasingly hostile crowd at bay. The mood began to get ugly, and people were beginning to panic.

Suddenly, near the front, a young student climbed onto his friend's shoulders and began to regale the crowd with witty comments and observations about what was going on. He performed like a stand-up comic. Everyone in the danger zone, including the police, was mesmerized by his performance. I could visibly see the tension decrease, the anger abate, the fears subside and a state of relative ease possess the crowd. The young man continued for over half-an-hour, using a superb weapon – humour – to save his fellows from probable serious injury.

the power of humour

Humour, like emotion, art and music, has often mistakenly been relegated to the 'weaker' mental skills. It is in fact one of the most powerful.

Consider the following:

A Force for Life

Laughter really *is* the best medicine! Norman Cousins, the famous author, was told that he had terminal cancer. Cousins refused to accept this absolute sentence, and immediately began to research the best cures and remedies, and chose his ultimate weapon ... humour!

He surrounded himself with cartoon books, humorous films, joke books and witty friends. The cancer did not stand a chance against the battering it took from the cannonballs of his belly laughs. He emerged from the hospital a healthier and a much, much happier man.

Humour and Sex

We are led to believe that bodies and their parts, including especially the eyes, lips, breasts, thighs and buttocks, and genitalia, are the prime sexual attractants.

However, all of these lose out to 'a sense of humour' – cited in survey after survey as the most sexually attractive trait. Why? Because laughter opens up both the mind and the senses, the prerequisites for intimacy and love-making.

Cartoons

These daily doses of visual and verbal humour are statistically among the most popular items that people around the world read in their daily newspapers. Senior editors of major national newspapers will tell you that even if only one of their regular popular cartoons is discontinued, the newspaper can lose tens of thousands of subscribers. When you smile or laugh, your brain instructs your body to release 'healthy hormones'. Cartoons are a daily humour dose equally as effective as 'an apple a day'!

Humour at War

What ultimate weapon do armies use? Humour! During wartime, forces spend millions of pounds putting on giant comedy tours, in which hundreds of thousands of soldiers and military workers are given regular 'energy injections' of wit and laughter. The global tours of Bob Hope to the American military are an outstanding case in point.

A number of armed forces are now specifically providing 'Happiness Training' to help protect their military personnel in the event of their capture.

The Wise Fool

Shakespeare, one of the most insightful writers of all time, realized that humour was one of the highest forms of intelligence. For this reason he regularly made the Fool in his plays not only the wittiest, but also the wisest of all the characters. He even said it explicitly in *Twelfth Night*: '*This fellow is wise enough to play the fool; And to do that well craves a kind of wit.*'

Comedians as Icons and Stars

Throughout history, comedians have been national and global stars, with a huge impact on popular culture. Think of the impact made by Charlie Chaplin, Danny Kaye, Laurel and Hardy, Bob Hope, Tony Hancock, Lucille Ball, Phil Silvers, Norman Wisdom, The Goons and the Monty Python team.

Millions of people regularly flock to comedians' shows and watch their television programmes and films, because they offer a vital ingredient in the brain's diet: laughter. Using their own Spiritual Intelligence, these geniuses stimulate that of many others. They help to put our worries and concerns into perspective, and by laughing with the comedians we can distance ourselves from our own preoccupations, seeing situations afresh – increasing our health, life expectancy and happiness!

Laughter Conquers Pain

Hospitals regularly report that they have far fewer complaints about pain when their patients are being entertained by people who make them laugh. Physiological studies also show that laughter increases the production of the body's own pain-killers, while at the same time increasing the strength of the immune system.

laughing your way to a happier, healthier and longer life

Dr Michael Miller, Director of the Center for Preventive Cardiology at the University of Baltimore, has found direct evidence that an active sense of humour may help prevent heart disease. The study showed that those who often laugh out loud and see the funny side of things, especially when situations are 'difficult', are far less likely to have a heart attack than more 'serious', unsmiling individuals.

The researchers used a questionnaire that assessed whether or not someone has enough *joie de vivre* to protect them from major or minor heart attacks and heart disease. The volunteers in the study were asked how they would respond to day-to-day situations such as arriving at a party to find someone else wearing the same outfit, or having soup dropped into their laps by a waiter.

Half of the people questioned had either suffered heart attacks or had been treated for clogged arteries. Their responses were compared with those of a control group, who were the same age but who had had no history of heart trouble.

The results were sombre for those less happy souls: the healthy group were 60 per cent more likely than their unhealthy counterparts to laugh in situations such as those described.

Doctors believe that laughter releases life-enhancing chemicals that help boost your immune system. A link has already been established, for example, between laughter and the antibodies which help ward off colds.

If you want to test your own laughter/health score, here are some questions based on Dr Miller's work. For each of the questions, any answer (a) scores 1 point; any answer (b) 2 points; any answer (c) 3 points; any answer (d) 4 points; and any answer (e) 5 points. Be honest with yourself – it might help to save your life!

1 **If you are watching a TV programme with friends that you found funny but nobody else did, how would you react?**
   (a) I would have concluded that I must have misunderstood it.
   (b) I would have smiled to myself, but the smile would not have reached my lips.
   (c) I would have smiled visibly.
   (d) I would have laughed aloud.
   (e) I would have laughed heartily.

2 **You are woken up late at night by an old friend phoning you, who is in town and is calling to say hello. Your friend is in a cheerful and bantering mood, cracking jokes. How would you react?**
   (a) I would not have been amused.
   (b) I would have felt amused but would not have laughed.
   (c) I would have been able to laugh at something funny my friend said.

(d) I would have been able to laugh *and* give some witty response.

(e) I would have laughed long and heartily with my friend.

3 You are eating out with friends when a waiter spills an ice-cold drink on you. How would you react?

(a) I would not be amused.

(b) I would be amused, but certainly would not show it outwardly.

(c) I would smile.

(d) I would laugh.

(e) I would laugh heartily.

4 The same as the situation above, except that this time the ice-cold drink is spilled on one of your friends. How would you react?

(a) I would not be amused.

(b) I would be amused but wouldn't show it.

(c) I would smile.

(d) I would laugh.

(e) I would laugh heartily.

The lower your score, the higher your risk of heart disease. The higher your score, the more your risk of heart disease will be reduced.

PoW Stories

A similar finding is coming to light from researches done around the world into survivors of the prisoner-of-war camps.

It seemed surprising at first (but in the light of our growing knowledge, it seems quite predictable), but that those who saw *only* the desperate and horrible side of their situation, were far less likely to survive than those who were able to see the ridiculous side as well. These second group were much more likely to survive in the long run.

Once again the explanation for this appears to lie in the chemicals released by the body when it is feeling humorous and 'bright', and similarly those restrictive chemicals released by the body when it is feeling 'down' and more hopeless.

'A man is happy so long as he chooses to be happy.'

(Alexander Solzhenitsyn)

tales of laughter

It is often assumed that Spirituality is a 'serious' business, and that humour and laughter have no part to play in a spiritually directed life. Happily, the opposite is true.

The false belief has come from the fact that people photographed in meditation or prayer can often appear 'serious' and because the qualities of Compassion, Understanding and Charity are usually related to the truly serious problems of other people's pain, hunger and suffering.

We tend to think of a spiritual person as someone not afraid to look at suffering, pain and death. It is in facing these things – and trying to alleviate that suffering – that a Spiritually Intelligent person turns toward laughter.

The Maharishi and Laughter

In the early 1970s, Peter Russell, from Cambridge University, was one of the first academics to study, in depth, meditation techniques and their effect on the body and mind. His main focus was on the newly-popular (thanks to The Beatles) Transcendental Meditation.

Peter reported a strange and enlightening thing: contrary to all expectations, the leader of the TM school, the Maharishi, laughed more than anybody else around him! While everyone else was trying to 'get' the 'secret', in front of them the Maharishi was demonstrating it second-by-second!

The Maharishi explained that if you could free your spirit, then it was obviously free to do the things it loved most, and one of those things was to laugh!

It is interesting to note that when someone is said to be 'spirited', we consider them full of the joys of life, constantly energetic and happy. We should keep this positive aspect of our Spiritual Intelligence uppermost in our (joyful) minds.

The Monster Game-Playing Computer

In 1992, the World Draughts/Chequers Champion, 65-year old Dr Marion Tinsley, who had only lost 5 games in 40 years, was challenged for the World Championship by a computer, programmed to calculate an incredible two million moves per second!

In all his pre-match interviews with the media, Dr Tinsley was amazingly relaxed and confident, regularly laughing and joking about the machine and its capabilities – capabilities that everyone else thought were unbeatable.

Throughout the 10-day, 40-game match, Dr Tinsley maintained his constantly upbeat and humorous persona, having both the members of the audience and interviewers in stitches with his unceasing wit and repartee.

When, having conquered the 'unbeatable machine', he finally won the match, he rose from his chair and, with a great beam on his face, lifted his hands to the skies and said: 'A victory for the Human Spirit!'

It's now time to 'uplift' *your* spirit with a Spiritual Workout!

spiritual workout

In this Spiritual Workout you will learn how to lighten up your mental attitude and your spiritual energy. You will emerge feeling spiritually refreshed, and with a much greater sense of fun and play.

1 Cultivate Fun Friends

Make sure that your circle of friends includes at least two who make you laugh. Try to include them regularly in your social events and parties, and be constantly on the lookout for new friends who are fun to be with.

2 Go to the Cinema or Theatre

Make a habit of going to see comedy films and plays, or to 'live' comedy clubs and allow yourself to have a really good belly-laugh, along with other members of the audience. This will act like a regular dose of medicine for you.

3 Smile and the World Smiles With You

Try the simple exercise of 'catching' people's eyes in the street as you walk past, and smiling at them. You will find that often even the most serious of faces will smile back.

4 Learn From the Prisoners of War

Even in the most horrible or dispiriting situations, try to keep, literally, your spirits up. If you do you will lessen the pain, ease your suffering and increase your chances of surviving the situation. Imagine re-telling your situation humorously – narrating the tale of a woeful date; a public humiliation thanks to something deeply embarrassing your child said or did; a spectacular blunder at work – as if it were a comedy sketch.

'He that loseth wealth, loseth much; he that loseth friends, loseth more; but he who loseth his spirit, loseth all.'

(Spanish Proverb)

5 Become a 'Laughter Doctor'

Knowing that laughter is good for your health, use your newly growing strengths of Compassion, Understanding and Charity to help others stay healthy by making them smile and laugh. Provide your friends and colleagues with opportunities for fun and laughter. Practise the art of joke telling, mimicking and comedy yourself.

Make sure you apply this medicine to yourself! Learn to laugh at yourself. This will give you new perspectives on who you are, and will add new dimensions to your personality while simultaneously enhancing your creativity.

6 Laughing Books

Assist yourself in the previous exercise by buying cartoon, joke and humorous books. These provide wonderful light interludes during the day or for night-time reading. They will regularly lift your own spirits, and will allow you to 'pass them on' to help lift the corners of the mouths and spirits of yourself and your friends.

7 Make Life Easy on Yourself!

Frowning requires a lot more muscular effort than smiling! A normal deep frown takes many more muscles than a normal big smile. Take the 'easy way out' and *smile*!

8 What Face to Wear?

Try frowning at a very young baby. Then try smiling. You will find that the baby will very often reflect your own expression. This reaction is not restricted to babies – it is a natural human trait!

Make a conscious decision as to what 'face' you present to the world, and what results you wish from that face.

9 Workout with a Laugh

Next time you really laugh, examine what is happening to your body as you do. Think of the kind of breathing involved, and what muscles are too. You will find that you are giving yourself one of the most complete physical workouts available!

From now on use Laughter as a form of physical exercise and as a health maintenance workout.

10 Do Something Fun

Take a 'circus skills flexibility course'; learn to belly-dance; try ice-skating – whatever you decide make it something different and exciting. Better still, try it with a group of friends!

spirit boosters

- I am an increasingly happy person, and smile whenever I have the opportunity.
- More and more I see the funny side of things and spread this 'good news' to my family and friends.
- I am usually cheerful, and bring a sense of lightness to my life and the lives of others.
- I am looking forward to a positive future for myself and the world.

- Surprising events and unusual outcomes delight my spirit. Such things bring a smile to my face and laughter to my heart.
- I love being in good and cheerful company and sharing laughter with my friends.

onward to the child's playground

chapter seven

' ... whoever does not receive the Kingdom of God like a child will never enter it.'

(Jesus of Nazareth)

Children are natural exponents of Spiritual Intelligence, and to boost our own spirituality we would do well to observe and learn from them.

This is not to say that we should revert to child*ish* behaviour, but rather that we should become more child*like* in our outlook, rediscovering those qualities with which we tend to lose touch the older we get, such as:

- boundless energy and enthusiasm
- unconditional love
- joyfulness
- spontaneity and excitement

- a sense of adventure
- openness and trust
- truthfulness
- generosity
- curiosity and inquisitiveness
- wonder and awe.

By opening ourselves up again to this way of looking at life, we increase dramatically our Spiritual Intelligence, as well as our sheer *joie de vivre*! In addition, our increased curiosity and enthusiasm will keep our minds and bodies healthy and active – and will help us to live longer, better-quality lives, packed with dynamism, fun and success.

You will finish this chapter having decided to discard childish attitudes (mean-spiritedness, spitefulness, etc.) and will have taken on board more spiritual, child*like* characteristics.

'Children are God's apostles, day by day
Sent forth to preach of love, and hope, and peace.'

(James Russell Lowell)

the best days of your life!

Why is childhood often referred to as idyllic?

The reason is that, fortunately for most of us, childhood is a time when we are living in a comparative spiritual paradise. We are living in an entirely new universe that is amazing to us; we are actively exploring all realms of knowledge and asking fabulously exciting and provocative questions; we are exploring our ethical systems, and working out 'how people work'; we are being loved and shown compassion by those closest and dearest to us; we are being given education and opportunity; we are exploring the wonderful worlds of laughter and enthusiasm; and we are being trained in ways that are valuable for our ongoing survival.

After this period of relative heaven come the increasing burdens of everyday life: bills, taxes, mortgages, grown-up responsibilities, injuries and illnesses, and the daily bombardment of bad news from the media.

Our problem as we mature is often not so much *what* happens to us, but how we *react* to it. We tend to become more serious and strict with ourselves; we punish ourselves for failures and lose our sense of play.

Happily, it is easy to reverse this trend to get back our childhood enthusiasm.

All you need to do is to decide that you are going to experience your 'second childhood'. The following stories show how this can be done:

Crabbing (But Not Crabby) in the Cold

Two families, with all their young and teenaged children, went to the seaside for a winter holiday. The children decided to go crabbing. Gathering their fishing lines they rushed off to the nearby pier and tossed them, bait-loaded, into the winter waves.

It was a cold, blustery day, and while the children were crabbing, their parents were walking along the windswept beach. One father,

---

a senior company executive, had been complaining about the weather and the cold, and was in a generally grumpy mood.

As they walked past the pier, he asked the others what the children were doing. On being told that they were crabbing, he decided to go and have a look, having never done such a thing when he was a child.

He went up to the children and asked them to explain to him what they were doing. Gleefully one of the little girls pulled up her line, which was festooned with four large crabs happily munching away on their meal.

'That's fantastic!' said the father. 'I've never done this before in my life – can I try?'

For the next four hours he was a child again, totally absorbed and lost in the magic and excitement of this new game, and completely oblivious of the weather. He returned home proudly brandishing his own cache, ruddy-faced and warm in body and spirit.

Crazes Are Not Crazy

Another family story again concerns a group on holiday. Yo-yos had once again become a popular craze, and the six children in the group all had their own new ones.

One of the fathers in the group was the managing director of an international bank. No matter where he was, and especially (horrifyingly) on family outings (because he had 'more time') he carried his briefcase with him. This was accompanied by his ubiquitous mobile phone, which went with him everywhere. He would constantly excuse himself when it rang, explaining that there were major international deals to which he just *had* to attend.

On the first afternoon of the holiday, the children brought out their yo-yos. The phone was doomed! This man, who on previous outings had been the most 'grey' and boring member of the group, was transformed when he saw the yo-yos come out.

He leapt up, and begged the children to lend him one of their toys. It turned out that as a child he had been the yo-yo king of his school.

For hour upon hour he displayed all his techniques, taught the children, and experimented with new yo-yo tricks. He sided with the children when they did not want to do things the other adults wanted them to, and his mobile phone, whenever it rang, was utterly ignored!

He had discovered, as children do, the *really* important things in life!

We all know why parents buy children certain toys – so that they, the parents, can play with them! We all remember the thrill of the fairground joyrides, the snowball fights, the games of charades, and the times spent lolling about in nature with *nothing* else to do but play, explore, create and daydream. My book *The Power of Creative Intelligence* contains far more information about the creative geniuses that are children.

childlike tales

Arthur Rubinstein and His 90ᵗʰ Birthdays!

When the famous concert pianist Arthur Rubinstein was celebrating his 90th birthday, a journalist asked him how it felt to be 90.

Rubinstein, famed for his childlike enthusiasm, replied that his 90th birthday day had felt just like any other. But 'just like any other' to Rubinstein was not 'just like any other' to most people!

He happily explained that each morning he had woken up, for his entire life, it had been as if each day was in fact a new birth. Rubinstein therefore considered that he had had $365 \times 90 = 32,850$ birthdays in his life to date!

As each day was a gift, he treasured it absolutely, knowing that it could be his last opportunity to marvel at the wonders and opportunities that it brought.

At the age of 90 Rubinstein felt as much like a child as he had ever done!

Another story concerning Arthur Rubinstein demonstrates even more dramatically his positive and childlike approach to life.

When he was in his later years, Rubinstein discovered that he was slowly going blind. A nervous journalist tentatively asked what effect this was having on his playing. The journalist obviously expected a considered, and perhaps melancholy response.

On the contrary, Rubinstein eagerly explained how before he had started to lose his sight he had always thought that he played the piano by ear only. Now that he was beginning to go blind, he realized that he had depended, far more than he had thought, on actually seeing his fingers flying over the keyboard, in the periphery of his vision.

Rather than being depressed and melancholic about this, Rubinstein was ecstatic!

He explained to the journalist how his new situation had opened up an entirely new world. He now had the fantastic opportunity of learning all these wonderful and beautiful pieces of music over again, *this* time by ear. He could hardly get over his excitement at having this wonderful new vista of learning open up to him.

Buckminster Fuller and His Child's Eyes

Buckminster Fuller, the American polymath who was a genius at nearly everything, was famous for his ability to see things with 'fresh' eyes. He changed the way the world looks at the weather, the Earth and the stars.

He would gleefully point out that wind does not blow Southwest

> – it sucks Northeast! And with similar childlike glee, he would
> report that the sun does not 'rise in the East'. It stays exactly where
> it is. The Earth rotates *towards* the sun, making it only appear as if
> it is rising.

I once shared a lecture-stage with Buckminster Fuller. At one point we had a brief break. He shot up to the Lecturers' Room before me, and when I arrived he was already sitting, cross-legged, a peaceful smile on his face, meditating.

After he had finished a little later, I asked him why he did this. He explained that it was to refresh his spirit and to give him more of that boundless (childlike!) energy that so characterized him.

'Every great and commanding movement in the annals of the world is the triumph of enthusiasm. Nothing great was ever achieved without it.'

(Ralph Waldo Emerson)

Tina Turner – The Child Who Wouldn't Retire!

Tina Turner, renowned throughout her long and distinguished singing career for her extraordinary energy, unquenchable spirit and bubbling childlike qualities, recently said of her future:

'I am much too creative a person to just go home and sit on the sofa. Now I can possibly do something different – I must be allowed to reinvent myself, to change ... Since I was a young child, I've

---

the power of spiritual intelligence

been gifted with the ability to make myself happy. I haven't
depended on someone else for that. I always gave a certain amount
of love to myself, because it wasn't always out there, and I've never
been one to draw on negative thoughts or bad memories. That's
why I am as happy as I am.'

some happy disturbing studies

Studies carried out by Dr Michael Miller in Florida in the 1990s,
focused on the link between the tendency to laugh and age. He came
up with the following soul-destroying statistics: the average six-year-old
child laughs 300 times a day. The average adult laughs only 47 times a
day – over six times less frequently! The more miserable the individual,
the less they laugh. The most miserable people managed to raise a
weak chuckle *less* than six times a day.

An even more disturbing study among 16,000 children, aged
between 3 and 15, was carried out by George Land and Beth Jarman.
This revealed how creativity, the spirit of adventure, curiosity and love
of learning new things – in other words, those Spiritually Intelligent,
childlike qualities – are gradually thwarted, crushed and buried over
the years.

The Spiritual Workout that follows is designed to help you break out
of your Spiritual bonds, and wake-up your childlike qualities again.

'Are you a God?' they asked the Buddha.
'No,' he replied.
'Are you an angel, then?'
'No.'
'A saint?'
'No.'
'Then what are you?'
Replied the Buddha: 'I am awake!'

spiritual workout

As you go through your workout, bear in mind the positive qualities of child*like*, as opposed to the petulant, selfish, jealous, angry, stubborn, pouting, bored, dissatisfied, disobedient and undisciplined characteristics of the child*ish*!

1 Variety is the Spice of Life

Introducing variety into all aspects of your life is a very good way to develop and maintain your childlike enthusiasm for things. Make a point of trying everything at least once – new foods, new hobbies, new places to visit. Become a connoisseur of experiences. Approach everything with a spirit of open enquiry – *expect* to find wonder and amazement in things – even, for example, if it is only the amazement that you finally plucked up courage to go bungee jumping!

2 Collect Moments of Contentment +

Moments of contentment should be sought after, recognized and appreciated. Looking at the world afresh through childlike eyes will help remind you of the things you have started to take for granted. The amount of enjoyment and total contentment children can glean from the simplest of things – hugging a teddy bear, watching a butterfly, playing with a straw in their drink – is amazing. Start to build your own moments of contentment! Notice when your cup of tea is just the right colour and temperature; when a stranger catches your eye and you share a smile; when you've finished the ironing and it is all crisp and clean smelling; when you've finally cleared your desk top and tidied up your papers; the unexpected sound of a bird singing in a lull of the daily noise around you. Gather these moments. Life is comprised of all these slices of Paradise; it is just up to you to enjoy them.

3 Cultivate a Playful Attitude

An attitude of play as you go about the things that you have to do is important for your spiritual development. It will also change how you feel about doing your tasks and chores! Funny as it may seem, it is only your attitude of boredom or disinterest that makes you feel down, and who is the loser here?

Consider how excited a child is to learn and then be allowed to help you do jobs about the house and garden. It is play for them – fun and exciting. And yes, you may feel that the one-millionth time of washing up the dishes is not so thrilling, yet there is still the potential for enjoyment. There is the satisfaction of seeing the stack of dirty dishes shrink and the clean pile grow; there is the opportunity to think, and to let your mind wander wherever it wants to.

You can look at all the 'boring' things you have to do in this light. Although your body may be stuck in a 'dreary' task, your mind is still free to see wonder and experience new opportunities at every turn.

'I know but one freedom and that is the freedom of the mind.'

(Antoine de Saint-Exupéry)

4 Be Cheerful!

Whatever there may be to cause unhappiness in your life, there is always the moment when you could choose to be cheerful. To start this process (if it feels a bit difficult) put on a 'happy face', smile, or just tweak your cheeks (this stimulates the brain to believe you are happy; it then produces happy chemicals, which make you happy!) Once you start this upward spiral it easily continues.

5 Keep an Open Mind

Keep an open mind and attitude about life. Have a positive expectation of events, and allow time to unfold and expose the reality. It is just possible that 'the other way' of doing something has greater benefits than the way you were intending.

6 Travel Light

Keep yourself light and unburdened – physically, mentally and materially – as you go through life. Children enjoy life, in part, because they do not usually carry a lot of 'baggage'. Dump yours! Start a gentle process of assessing any excess baggage – old ideas, mind sets – that you do have, and then consider how to get rid of it.

Mentally you are already progressing as you reflect and act on the suggestions in this book. However, an attitude of lightness is most important. This does not say that you do not care about things – only that it does not help any situation to be 'heavy' about it! Most things that you worry and fret about never came about. What a waste of time! And if they did happen just as you feared, the worry has not helped; it just made you less able to deal with the actual emergency. So consider if there is something you need to do, and do it, but remain light and bright.

7 Remember Your Natural Childlike Generosity

Young children love to share, love to help, love to give. That generous nature is alive and well in you, so reconnect with it and *give*! Give freely, without any strings attached.

8 Keep Flexible!

Can you put your toe in your mouth? Well, you *were* able to once! There are two aspects to flexibility, the physical and the mental. At a physical level, maintaining a flexible and supple body is the secret of 'eternal youth': it protects you from injury, and lets your energy flow through you easily. Try beginning a gentle stretching programme – Yoga or Tai Chi classes are among the best ways to become more supple.

A flexible mind *also* gives eternal youth! You are already exploring openness of thought and curiosity; link these with flexibility. Look at the alternatives, try things a different way; it keeps things fresh, adds fun, and may give you a whole new idea – '*necessity is the mother of invention*'. Flexible thinking keeps your brain agile: enjoy the rewards.

9 Dance!

'Dance should be a divine expression of the human spirit.'

(Isadora Duncan)

Frolicking and dancing are the natural expressions of the child, and the natural expressions of the high-spirited human being. Dance promotes flexibility of body and mind; it is a wonderful aerobic exercise, and it encourages the expression of your joy and laughter.

10 Live Each Day

Be like Arthur Rubinstein, and consider every day of your life to be a new 'birthday'. Celebrate it as such! Remember that if you live to be 100 (which in these days is becoming more and more probable), you have 36,500 birthdays to celebrate!

spirit boosters ✦

- I celebrate my childlike qualities, and continue to strengthen them.
- I am playful and adventurous.
- I am an increasingly happy and enthusiastic person, spreading my happiness and enthusiasm to others.
- I am a dancer, and move with joy and enthusiasm.
- I love my senses, and use them constantly to 'see' familiar things in new ways.

chapter eight

'Does not every true man feel that he is himself made higher by doing reverence to what is really above him?'

(Thomas Carlyle)

The word 'Ritual' comes from the Latin *ritus*, which means a custom or a way of doing something.

Rituals generally have a form: they are bounded by time and space and involve creating a special place or sacred environment, in which the ritual, or meaningful gesture or ceremony takes place. Rituals are often performed in a prescribed order, which have often passed down from generation to generation. Rituals can also be private, personal and highly individual: for example, taking time to stop and admire the view every time you walk over a certain bridge.

Rituals can be observed just once or they can be common traditions passed down through the ages (from festivals celebrating the change of seasons to religious rites, or to using your Grandmother's special shortbread or cake recipe every Christmas). All of us participate in rituals, whether we are aware of it or not. If you've ever attended a wedding, observed a national holiday or day of remembrance, or even sent a Valentine's card, then you have experienced first-hand the power of Ritual.

Rituals work on a level that is beyond the personal. They connect us to the past and to something bigger than ourselves: be it a force of nature, a social event or the divine. One example is Valentine's day. This originated as a Roman fertility rite, but has now come to mean a time to express romantic love and affection. In its original form it commemorated something much greater than mere sentiment – it was a way to celebrate new life and honour the life force, something essential to the continuity of the community.

Rituals also connect us to our deepest selves and to each other.

This chapter will show you the incredibly positive effect Ritual can have on you, your brain and your life; you will discover how to enhance your Spiritual Intelligence (and your overall intelligence!) through the power of Ritual.

community rituals

Rites of Passage

Rites of passage and initiation are probably the public rituals with which we are most familiar – weddings, naming ceremonies, graduations, house warmings, funerals, birthdays and anniversaries –

those rituals, serious or fun (or both), which mark important occasions in our lives.

Such rituals help to ground and centre us, and give us a sense of belonging to our wider communities. One wonderful example is that of an Amish barn-raising – where the entire village come together to build a house for a newly married couple. Other such rituals are those traditional 'coming of age' or 'initiation rites'. These rituals are designed to mark the transition from childhood or adolescence into adulthood and adult rights and responsibilities.

Days of Rest

'Some keep the Sabbath going to Church –
I keep it staying at Home –
With a Bobolink for a Chorister –
And an Orchard for a Dome.'

(Emily Dickinson)

One ritual that is at the heart of our calendar is Sunday as a day of rest, a tradition passed down from the Bible. To have one day in the week when you put *all* your work aside and just spend the day relaxing makes for good mental and physical health. This is something we can try to do whether we are religious or not. And it doesn't have to be Sunday – it can be any day in the week ritually dedicated to rest.

Traditionally, Sunday is a time when families and friends have gathered together for a Sunday lunch and a walk in the park or religious observation.

The Ritual of Remembrance

'A man's dying is more the survivor's affair than his own.'

(Thomas Mann)

One of the most familiar public remembrance rituals is the annual Remembrance Day or Poppy Day services, which are held on the same day in November, at the same hour, not just all over the country, but throughout most of the world. This started as a way to honour and remember the millions of dead of the First World War, on all sides of the conflict, and has grown to commemorate the dead of subsequent wars and conflicts.

Despite its public nature, Remembrance Day is often a personal Ritual of remembrance for many, many people – a time to remember loved ones, regardless of whether they died in war or not. Such private remembrance rituals can also consist of laying flowers at someone's grave on special anniversaries.

Loved one's don't have to be dead to be remembered in a Ritual – the tradition of drinking to absent friends is also an act of remembrance.

the power of spiritual intelligence

strengthening your inner strength

The accelerating pace, the increasing chaos and the growing bombardment of information that now form the basic fabric of 'modern life' keep us away from spiritual thoughts and activities, while at the same time making us yearn for them even more.

Even the home can become an anti-sanctuary, with household chores mounting up, the dog whining for a walk, or the children wanting more and more of your time and energy. You can't even relax in front of the TV because of all the doom and gloom which spews out of it!

How *do* you escape from the 'madding crowd'?

Where *do* you find spiritual peace and revitalization?

Where do you find your sanctuary?

Through Ritual!

Ritual can be considered a hearth to which you go for warmth, rest and regeneration. By its very nature it gives you order, stability, security and certainty in the turbulence that often swirls around you. Ritual allows your mind and spirit to be secure in the knowledge that within its 'space' there'll be little threat of disruption.

In the space that Ritual provides for you, you can become more involved in the thoughts and actions that allow you to enter more fully into your Spiritual being.

Furthermore, Ritual is an inherent part of the nature of humankind and spirituality – every tribe, group or nation throughout history have included the constancy of Ritual as part of their social fabric. Such rituals always involve thinking about or vocalizing spiritual concepts, and the contemplation of and involvement with nature.

In most instances Ritual was connected to various forms of transcendence, in which people as individuals or in mass groups were able to override the pain, suffering and grief that was gripping them, and to add to their own individual energies those of others, the world and the universe that surrounded them.

It is interesting to observe that in all societies, when stress becomes too much, people will often retreat into Ritual as the ultimate form of defence, using the manic cleaning of things and the body, or the similarly manic ordering of the environment, as a 'last stand' against the tidal-waves of troubles that are assaulting their souls.

Ritual can be considered one of the main methods of cleansing 'noise pollution' from our minds. Even such simple, regular activities as walking the dog, working in the garden, or simply taking a break, can provide us with that regular order and stability that allows us to shut out the aggravations and demands surrounding us, and to enter into a more elevated form of communication with ourselves, others and nature.

An increasing number of people pursuing Spiritual Intelligence are creating 'locations' in their home that are their spiritual 'spots'. They go to these on a regular basis, to regain whatever balance had been lost in the hours before.

One friend of mine has made the bath her 'spot'. Usually once a day she has a warm bath suffused with aromatic oils. The only light is that from candles. As she describes it:

'As soon as I begin to slip into the water the millions of voices screaming for attention in my head immediately begin to subside and one voice only becomes more and more dominant – *my* Inner Voice. As I sink in I begin to feel my diaphragm open up and become more free, my breathing relaxes and becomes more deep and regular, and my entire body becomes more quiet, still, easy and at peace with itself. As soon as I am submerged I am bathed not only by the warm water, oils and perfumes, but also by the power that self-reflection gives me.

'It is private time. It is precious time. It is my own time. It is my time with *Me*.'

As you have been becoming increasingly aware throughout the pages of *The Power of Spiritual Intelligence*, more and more people are heading out onto the spiritual highways.

lessons from the gurus

The Indian Yogis are amongst the most revered of the spiritual leaders and teachers in the world. Long before the advent of modern civilization the Yogis had discovered the immense power of spiritual and physical rituals. They used these rituals to train their bodies and minds during their quests for spiritual enlightenment.

Similarly, practitioners of the Asian martial arts – kung-fu, karate, tae kwan do – use 'Correct Ritual' to train their minds and bodies on their paths to disciplined enlightenment.

your brain cells love ritual!

Some exciting new research about the value of Ritual comes from the 'good news' centre: the Brain Front! The expression 'Practice makes Perfect' has been around for many years, and is generally true (although it doesn't work if the practice is the wrong kind of practice – this just makes you worse!)

Researchers wanted to know why this was so, and during the past 20 years have come up with the most extraordinary discovery. As we saw in Chapter 2, every action you take lays down a *pathway in your brain*! This pathway, like a new track across a field, gets stronger and more defined the more you go over (repeat) the thought or activity.

This applies to physical training rituals, but it also applies to repeating rituals of prayers or mantras or meditations – and even to repeating rituals of tradition like special meals or family celebrations.

By repeating rituals and activities, they become *habits*.

By finding the 'Right Rituals', you increase the probability that you will be able to overcome obstacles and endure difficulties with a much lighter spirit and greater probability of success.

It's time for your Spiritual Workout!

spiritual workout

Knowing that positive Rituals ingrain good habits in your brain, and strengthen you against the 'slings and arrows of outrageous fortune', it is obviously sensible to incorporate them into your life in as many ways as you can.

As you prepare to develop your own Spiritually enhancing Rituals, be aware of the fact that Rituals are a very efficient way of improving yourself and your Spiritual Intelligence. They get rid of the waste-of-time-necessity of 'starting all over again'. They also give you great comfort – you can snuggle into your Rituals like a favourite old sweater.

Below are some exercises to help you establish your own personal Rituals to help you through your day.

1 Mind-Map®

Mind-Map® all those areas of your life where Ritual could be used to enhance it, both generally and Spiritually. As you develop this Mind-Map®, make sure that you do not use Ritual to rigidify your life, but be aware of the time-saving aspect of Ritual. Remember, Ritual should be used to expand your life and make it more flexible and more successful.

2 Have a Ritual of Thanks at Mealtimes

Take just a minute or two to have a Ritual of thanks before you eat any meal. Give thanks for all the people involved in getting that meal to your table. Consider those who grew the food; harvested it; packaged it; transported it; sold it; bought it; prepared it; and for your body, which will digest the food to keep you alive and well.

3 The Dawn Ritual

Each day is a fresh start! Use Ritual to prepare yourself and your spirit for the day ahead. Start your days with some soothing music, or five minutes of meditation to set yourself up for the tasks ahead, or some gentle stretching to wake up your body and mind. For four years in my early 20s, I started my own days with the wonderful dawn music of the Peer Gynt Suite – it made the sun rise in my mind, no matter what the weather outside!

Be aware, at the beginning of the day, of the ever-present gifts of love, friendship, peace, wisdom, nature and life that you have, and slip into these as you slip into your clothes. Carry them with you for the day.

4 The Meeting/Greeting Ritual

The 'first times' are extremely important for you and for other people. Your brain will automatically remember such first meetings better than subsequent ones.

Make sure, therefore, that when you say 'hello' to people, you make it a positive high point – a happy-snapshot in their memory banks! Make the 'positive start' a permanent Ritual in your Spiritual Intelligent behaviour.

5 The Leaving/Departing Ritual

Just as your brain will remember the 'first things', so it will remember the 'last things'. So it is very important to make sure that your 'farewells' are positive – as you will be remembered through them.

Check this for yourself – do you *remember* the last time you saw the person you love the most?

Get into the habit of always saying 'goodbye' with a smile – and think, 'What if I never saw this person again, and this were the last memory we would each have of each other?' Act from that thought, and create a Departure Ritual that leaves both of you in a spiritually uplifted frame of mind.

Is it not nicer to walk away with a spring in your step and a smile in your thoughts?!

6 End-of-the-Day Ritual

Going to sleep is already a Ritual that you have established throughout your life! You can make it an even more positive one!

At the end of the day, just before going to sleep, your mind is in a particularly open state. It is therefore a good idea to 'fill it' with good thoughts and imaginings, and with things that can help you in your own personal and Spiritual growth.

It is very beneficial to establish the Ritual of running over the day in your mind, checking as much as you can of what happened. You can use this time to reflect on the lessons learned during the day, and to incorporate them into your ongoing life.

On the basis of your review of the day, you can then image and envision the general goals and plans for the next day, leaving you with a feeling of anticipation and expectation rather than, as often happens after a tough day, a feeling of exhaustion, depression and dread about the day to come!

Even on those 'tough days' there are many gifts that you have been given, so look for them and fall asleep counting your blessings, rather than sheep!

7 The Perfect Service Ritual

In this Ritual you hold the thought 'Perfect Service' in mind as much as you can as you go about your daily life. Everything you do, for yourself or for others, do as excellently as you can, including such simple things as making a cup of tea, cleaning the bird cage, giving someone the time, preparing a meal, making the bed or driving a car, etc. Just think of a Japanese Tea Ceremony! Do *everything* with attention and care. Always consider that you are doing it for somebody who is extra-special (you are regardless of whether it's yourself or someone else!), and put love into the job.

This Ritual makes it much more enjoyable for you to do whatever you have to do, and makes the receiver of your 'services' happier and more spiritually uplifted than if you had not cared so much.

8 Mark Your Rituals

Mark your Rituals in some symbolic way. Light a candle or incense stick when you begin a Ritual of meditation, or have a minute or two's silent thanksgiving at the start of a special family meal. Such acts allow you to separate your time of Ritual from your normal activities, and are a great way of cleansing your thoughts and concentrating your mind.

9 Create a Ritual Space

You can create a sacred space for yourself wherever you are. At work you could simply put up a postcard, or write out a saying, which you find brings out a spirit of reverence in you. You can make a Ritual of looking at this in times of stress and using it to 'anchor' you to a more expansive state. Or you can create a 'portable sacred space' by carrying something like a special stone, photograph or symbol (a cross, a key, a labyrinth) with you throughout your day and when you travel, transporting your sacred space to an ordinary hotel room. You could also create a sacred space in your garden, a particular spot where you can sit and contemplate.

10 Meditate/Rest Ritual

Practise a short meditation or restful Ritual every day, to help your Spiritual well-being and health. The next chapter deals comprehensively with this entire subject.

spirit boosters

- I create time to mark and celebrate the important moments in life.
- I embrace personal daily Rituals to help keep me centred.
- I constantly use Ritual to move reality closer to my dreams.
- I am committed to my vision. Every day I strengthen my resolve, through Ritual, to accomplish it.

peace

chapter nine

**'If there is righteousness in the heart,
there will be beauty in the character.
If there is beauty in the character,
there will be harmony in the home.
If there is harmony in the home,
there will be order in the nation.
If there is order in the nation,
there will be peace in the world.'**

(Confucius)

Peace is that state of stillness or calm in which there is freedom from anxiety, disturbance and distress. Perhaps the best metaphor is that of a tranquil pond or lake where no ripples or rough winds disturb the surface.

Peace is a state that can exist within an individual, a household, a neighbourhood, a country and a world. The startling truth is that the more individuals who are at peace with themselves, the greater is the probability that all communities, local and global, will also be peaceful.

'Where people are praying for peace the cause of peace is being strengthened by their very act of prayer, for they are themselves becoming immersed in the spirit of peace.'

(John Macquarrie)

Both a peaceful being and a focus on peaceful behaviour have been the hallmarks of all the great spiritual leaders – from Buddha and Christ to Mahatma Gandhi. Despite great personal suffering and sacrifices, these teachers managed to maintain their inner peace; the real test of how at peace people are within themselves, is just how they cope with the adversity and turmoil around them.

'Peace comes not by establishing a calm outward setting so much as by inwardly surrendering to whatever the setting.'

(Hubert van Zeller)

We are increasingly living in a 24-hour-day, seven-day-week, no-breaks-allowed society, addicted to mobile phones, the internet, computers, video screens and *noise*. More and more people are internally (and some externally!) screaming: '*Stop the world – I want to get off!*'

This chapter will show you how!

In order to establish peace within yourself, and to bring about that 'tranquil lake' state, it is essential that you learn how to reduce disturbance in your life, lessen anxiety and eliminate stress. This will allow your body, mind and soul to live in an internal environment that is calm and serene. It is from this inner calmness that you can then bring your peace out into the world.

peace and meditation

Meditation is defined as a period of time spent focusing one's mind for spiritual purposes or as a relaxation method. In *The Power of Spiritual Intelligence* we will use the full range of definitions, including 'blank mind' meditations, prayer, focusing on specific problems to gain solutions, self-programming meditations, communing with nature, and rest and relaxation.

By understanding the importance of providing yourself with internal silence and rest, you will come to understand the value of the meditation techniques that have been spreading so rapidly and beneficially around the world. These 'Stress Busters' clear the clutter that is in your mind, give you a new sense of serenity and calm, and (as many people report) put you more 'in touch with the Cosmos'.

The Great Spiritual Leaders and Meditation

It is interesting and very motivating to note that the great spiritual leaders, without exception, both practised and promoted meditation as a means of gaining physical, mental and spiritual health, as well as the prime method for gaining wisdom and enlightenment.

A quick survey itself proves enlightening!

1 Moses (c.1300 BC)

Moses was renowned as a deep thinker who spent long periods 'soul searching' while tending his father-in-law's sheep in the hills. The fourth Commandment – 'Remember the Sabbath day ...' – specifically states that at least one day per week should be devoted to rest and relaxation.

2 Mahavira (c.599–527 BC)

A thousand years after Moses, and more than 7,000 miles away, Mahavira explored a spiritual path in which he followed many forms of meditation. The spiritual path that Mahavira began, Jainism, involves set periods of meditation, as well as precepts against harming any and all sentient beings. For example, adherents wear gauze masks over their mouths, so they won't breathe in and kill any insects.

3 Buddha (c.563–483 BC)

One of the most widespread images of Buddhism is that of Buddha seated in meditation. 'Buddha' means 'the awakened one', and it was through meditation that he became utterly *awake* – to everything.

Two of the foundation-stones for Buddha's Noble Eightfold Path – his formula for leading an increasingly spiritual life – are 'Right Contemplation': 'One must always learn to control the mind in peaceful contemplation ...'; and 'Right Concentration': 'When all the other principles have been followed, one can reach the state where the mind is completely subject to one's will. One can develop the mind to heights beyond reasoning, indeed to Nirvana.'

Nirvana is the state of complete detachment from unnecessary cravings, and a state of absolute, transcendent peace.

4 Confucius (551–479 BC)

Confucius (Kung-fu tze) is still reverently referred to by the Chinese as 'the First Teacher'. As a young boy he was known as a 'Child of Nature' – one who spent much time in questioning and contemplation.

In his teachings Confucius emphasized that meditation was a necessary part of self-development.

Among his dictums for leading a good and spiritual life were the following:

- Good people examine themselves.
- Good people cautiously practice introspection.
- Good people can stand alone without fear and can leave society without distress.
- Good people strengthen themselves ceaselessly.
- Good people shine with the quality of enlightenment.

5 Jesus (AD 0–33)

At the beginning of his ministry, Jesus spent 40 days and nights in the desert wilderness, alone with the wild animals, meditating and preparing himself, mentally and spiritually, for his calling.

Throughout his life and work, Jesus would regularly retreat into the hills and countryside to spend time alone in prayer and thought. He taught that this 'direct communication with God' could and should be done by anyone, in any place, at any time.

6 Muhammad (AD 570–632)

The Prophet Muhammad founded one of the fastest growing spiritual movements in the world – Islam (which means 'peace'!)

Muhammad considered Meditation and Prayer to be so important that they form a major part of the first of his Five Pillars of Islam:

'You must meditate and pray five times a day: on arising, when the sun reaches its zenith, its mid-decline, sunset and before retiring.'

practical steps to gain peace

Rest and Relaxation

According to numerous studies, taking rest breaks or siestas for half-an-hour or so during the day works far better and far faster than caffeine in increasing alertness, and decreasing tiredness and stress.

One particularly interesting study of workers in industrial and post-industrial nations suggested that meditating, resting or taking a nap increased the productivity, creativity and problem-solving skills of 92.5 *per cent* of the workers! The study suggests that we do not so much need coffee breaks – we need meditation breaks!

Another study conducted on American soldiers had similar results. It showed that those soldiers who were given a 30-minute rest and relaxation break were far more able to make 'critical decisions based on attention to detail' than those who had to rely on several cups of coffee alone.

Meditation Techniques

There are many different types of meditation – standing meditation, moving meditation, sitting meditation, transcendental meditation and chant meditation, among others. Some concentrate on emptying the mind, others on developing a trance-like state of altered consciousness, while others (especially the moving meditations of Tai Chi and Chi Chung) involve exercising the external and internal body at the same time. Still others, such as Christian meditation and some forms of Jewish meditation focus on chanting or reflecting on specific holy texts.

The starting point of almost all types of meditation is, however, the *breath* and *breathing*. A very simple, easy meditation you can try is to sit comfortably somewhere quiet, close your eyes, and concentrate on slowly breathing, in and out. Some people like to count their breaths, going up to ten and then returning to one. They can then notice if their mind has wandered. If they lose their place, they simply return to one, without feeling guilty for being distracted. They let the thoughts go and return to the breath.

As you concentrate on your breathing, the thoughts chasing through your mind will gradually subside, and you will end your meditation feeling relaxed, refreshed and alert.

'If the heart wanders or is distracted, bring it back to the point quite gently ... and even if you did nothing during the whole of your hour [of contemplation]

but bring your heart back, though it went away every time you brought it back, your hour would be very well-employed.'

(St. Francis de Sales)

My Personal Meditation Experiments

Like most people I know, I had many meditative experiences as a child: sitting by ponds or streams and being transported by the hazy and sleepy rhythms of nature; or 'meditating' in class when I was supposed to be paying attention to the teacher!

My first formal contact with meditation came when studying Yoga, and contemplating various parts of my body (some being easier to do than others!) I also experimented with a number of different Zen Buddhist forms of meditation, focusing on chants. These I found particularly soothing and calming, while at the same time invigorating.

When The Beatles introduced the Maharishi Mahesh Yogi and Transcendental Meditation to the world in the mid-1960s a friend taught me this form of meditation. In it you simply repeat a mantra over and over again, using it to clear your mind of any other intruding thoughts. I can report from personal experience that this form of meditation truly does make you feel 'light'. I also learnt deep relaxation and self-hypnosis techniques. This transformed my life, enabling me both to 'see' different levels of my consciousness simultaneously, and to direct my will and intention, incredibly powerfully.

The high point of my own meditation career thus far occurred in Mexico in the last year of the last millennium. On a beautifully sunny, autumn day, a group of Mexican artists, writers and students of Spiritual Intelligence invited me to visit the giant pyramid temple of Teotihuacán. We climbed the dizzying heights to its peak, and surveyed the pre-Mayan landscape.

When we were descending, a guide appeared out of nowhere, and asked if we would like to visit the Meditation Chamber, a privilege not usually reserved for tourists such as myself.

We eagerly accepted the invitation, and were taken, through a 'secret' gate, into an underground tunnel that was sometimes so small we had to get down on all fours to make our way. Lit only by torchlight, we eventually came to the Meditation Chamber: a small opening some 20 feet underground and hundreds of feet below the point of the pyramid. We were at the 'heart' centre of the pyramid's base!

Our guide had us stand in a circle, hold hands, close our eyes, and meditate on the silence and 'feel' of the energy in this magical spot that had been a private Meditation and Prayer Chamber for the priests of this magnificent temple.

The feeling was so calming, so strengthening, and we felt so 'at one' with Everything, that none of us wanted to leave. Ever!

spiritual workout

1 Discover the Power and Energy in Silence and Meditation

It is very easy to do, and wonderful to experience as a family, or with friends. The great thing about Silence and Meditation is that you can do it anywhere and you require no extra equipment!

2 Spread Peace Around You!

Join with other people and project your inner peace out to the wider world. Commit to joining others to spread peace and peacefulness wherever you go.

3 A Peaceful Start to Your Day

Most people wake up in a hurry and never stop rushing until they go to bed again!

Start the day calmly, more peacefully and more in control of yourself, your feelings and what is fed into your head. Before you fully wake up, gently review your dreams (if you can remember them), check how you feel at the moment, what particular mood you are already in and how you can steer that to your advantage during the course of the day. Develop a morning ritual of gentle stretching and pleasant sounds (bird song or calm, relaxing music) to introduce you to your new 'birth' day, every day!

4 Turn Everything Off!

Have a 'silent' moment – or two – preferably at the same time every day. No television blaring, or radio, no equipment running, just as much silence as you can. Start with a few minutes and slowly increase the time. If you are living in a noisy neighbourhood get some earplugs, or some 'white noise tapes'; they balance out noise and give your ears silence.

A more challenging exercise would be to practise peacefulness sitting in a traffic queue or at the supermarket checkout!

5 'Traffic Control'

About mid-morning, mid-afternoon and mid-evening, set aside a time to STOP whatever you are doing. If you can have some quiet, relaxing music playing just for a couple of minutes, do so. If not, imagine it playing in your head. After a few minutes, continue with your life. If possible get those around you to do the same; it changes the atmosphere and energy of your environment for the better.

6 Make Your Home Your Sanctuary

Truly consider your home to be your Peace and Creativity Centre. Check your environment and activities at home. Create, for example, a TV-free zone. Resolve not to listen to/watch *all* the news bulletins (when did they ever give good news?!)

If you have children, you will know that children become more fractious, irritable and disobedient if they hop from one form of entertainment to another (Nintendo® to TV to computer to Game Boy®, etc.) They are normally far more pleasant, happy and calm if left to potter, read and be with themselves in their own imaginations and fantasies. Make sure that they have space to do 'nothing'.

Work actively to make your home a 'calm' in the centre of the storm.

7 Check Out Different Forms of Meditation

There are many different forms of meditation, and some suit some people better than others. It is worth spending some time gently checking the options, and eventually choosing those paths which are most meaningful and beneficial for you. Almost all traditional religions have some form of meditation practice – from Sufi whirling, through Buddhist walking meditation, to Christian contemplative forms. On the way you will meet many new and interesting friends.

8 Learn from the Great Spiritual Teachers

Seek out the sayings of the great Spiritual teachers, and learn from their words and examples. They are wonderful role models and will offer you many interesting options and opportunities in your own search for the Truth.

9 Dance Meditation

In the peace and sanctuary of your home, spend some time listening to beautiful, flowing, peaceful and rhythmical music, letting your body express itself in any way it feels, and letting your mind either wander 'free' or focus on some particular aspect of your life. Or try out some 'trance dance' sessions, or even various Native dancing ceremonies.

10 Spend Time with Animals and Nature

Many animals live in a constant meditative state: relaxed alertness. Spend time with them; communicate with them; learn from them! If you have problems that are unsettling your Peace of mind, go for a long walk in the country by yourself or with a friend, and walk and work it out!

11 Meditate in Your Life

Any activity can be turned into a meditation. Try an 'eating meditation': do nothing but fully attend to your chocolate bar or entire meal. When bathing, bathe consciously and with awareness, rather than making up a to-do list of what's to come in the day ahead.

> **'Every path, every street in the world is your walking meditation path.'**

(Thich Nhat Hanh)

spirit boosters

- I choose Peace for myself and all living beings.
- I am increasingly calm, centred and Peaceful.
- I am incorporating the Rituals of Meditation more and more into my daily life.
- I am increasingly calm and patient, allowing the fruits of my actions to ripen in the fullness of time.
- I heal myself, gently returning to equilibrium and balance, nurtured by my inner peace.
- I remain steady in the midst of complexity and sure in times of distress.
- Today I invite into my Body, Mind and Spirit a higher level of awareness.
- With great calm I observe the flow of my mind, then welcome inner silence.
- I increasingly feel in touch with the Cosmos, its grandeur, its magnificence and its beauty.

all you need is love!

chapter ten

'Love is patient and kind; it is not jealous or conceited or proud; love is not ill-mannered or selfish or irritable; love does not keep a record of wrongs; love is not happy with evil, but is happy with the truth. Love never gives up; and its faith, hope, and patience never fail.'

(St. Paul, First Letter to the People of Corinth)

'Spread love everywhere you go: first of all in your own house. Give love to your children, to your wife or husband, to a next door neighbour ... Let no one ever come to you without leaving better and happier.'

(Mother Teresa)

'Love' is defined as a feeling of great and deep affection and interest. It gives those who love intense pleasure in caring for and contemplating the object of their Love. It has the power to heal, comfort, empower, conquer, inspire and,

ultimately, to give life.

'Love is the only force capable of transforming an enemy into a friend.'

(Martin Luther King)

Conversely, the absence of Love can cause anxiety, depression, pain, suffering, despair, hopelessness, illness, disease and, ultimately, death.

The Love of self, others and the Universe can be regarded as the ultimate Life and Spiritual Goal.

The origins of the word 'love' can be found in the ancient German and English 'leof', meaning 'dear' and 'pleasant', and sounding very similar to the word 'life'! In one sense, therefore, we can truly say that 'Life is Love' and 'Love is Life'!

This final chapter will introduce you to the Ultimate Power – the Power of Love. I will tell you stories of adventure, despair, death and hope, and hopefully guide you towards some approaches for easing pain, suffering and despair. You should leave the chapter with a sense of openness, understanding and compassion, and be inspired to develop this power within yourself, both for your benefit and for that of your family, friends and the common good.

'Love seeketh not itself to please,
Nor for itself hath any care,
But for another gives its ease,
And builds a Heaven in Hell's despair.'

(William Blake)

love and fear

Love is the antidote to the state that is behind almost all negative emotions – _fear_. Fear is a result of a sense of separation– from others, from the rest of life – and love is a result of being alive to our connectedness. If we can train ourselves to use the power of love to conquer fear, then we take a giant step towards greater Spiritual Intelligence.

'Taking and Sending'

Our natural inclination is to try to distance ourselves from fear and to get as much love for ourselves as possible. This reaction is based on our basic survival fears. In Tibet and elsewhere, they try to cultivate the opposite reaction with a profoundly transformative meditation practice of 'taking and sending'. In this, rather than trying to take love, the meditators endeavour to 'send' it to others. Rather than run from fear, they try to take on the burden of fear others may feel.

To 'take and send' you envision breathing in the fear and suffering of another (say if you see someone on the street who is struggling to walk), and then breathe out your own love, joy and contentment. You turn negativity into positive energy radiated towards another. It is a very subtle practice, but it enhances our ability to generate selfless love and to see ourselves in others. It also changes our relationships with others and the world itself.

the practical power of love

A story will help illustrate the powerful effects of love. Make sure that you spread its positive qualities around!

The Story of the Beautiful Fish

Those who have read my book *Head First* will know how rabbits that are given positive affection and Love while in captivity were healthier and lived longer than those rabbits which were merely fed and watered adequately. This story of the beautiful fish confirms how a little love goes a very long way!

When I was a young boy my main interest was nature and the study of its processes and wonders. I used to breed entire menageries, including butterflies, amphibians, fish and rabbits.

One of the most beautiful things I had ever seen was the male three-spined stickleback. This tiny, streamlined animal looked like the essence of 'fishness'. In the mating season the body of the male is a translucent, almost luminescent steel-blue, with a throat and underbelly that is a vibrant blush-red.

I used to breed these wondrous little creatures in a giant aquarium, and each male would stake out its territory, building nests of weeds and rushes in which they incubated the young. One summer day I caught the biggest, most beautifully luminescent male I had ever seen.

I gently introduced it to the aquarium, expecting it to stake out its own territory (probably slightly bigger than the rest, because of the fish's size and magnificence). To my surprise, it did not do so. It swam rapidly into a cluster of weeds at the surface of the aquarium, and tried to avoid the occasional 'raids' from the other males.

I expected nature would look after itself, and for a natural balance of power to establish itself by the following day. But the fish was still in its same place the next morning. It had become slightly less radiant, seemed to be a little timid, and was still avoiding attacks from the other males.

Day-after-day I found the 'magnificent' stickleback still in the same place, increasingly less colourful, increasingly timid and increasingly attacked. After five days the little fish had become a grey and dull colour, and I began to fear for his life.

The only thing I could think of to do was to nurture and care for him. I began to stroke him gently, to let him know that there was no threat from me, and at feeding times made sure that he had just that little bit extra. I also gave him more weeds in which to protect/defend himself.

Within two days I was *just* able to detect a slight change in his colouring: he was becoming a little more radiant! Day-by-day I showered him with the only manifestations of love available to me, and day-by-day his spirit returned.

Within a week he was back to his full magnificence, and began to make sorties outside his weed-home territory. Within a fortnight he had established his own 'home area' in the aquarium, and nature *had* looked after itself.

The stunning realization to me was that 'nature looking after itself' was not about size, strength, beauty or magnificence; all these had meant nothing to my stickleback. Nature looking after itself *included* me, and, more importantly, included the Power of Love.

It was the Power of Love that had triumphed over everything.

love and science

Did you know that a good shopkeeper can tell, however hard you try to conceal it, that you Love some*thing* or some*one*?

How?

They look at your eyes!

Why?

Because, when you look at something or someone that you love, your eyes open – *wide*!

Your brain wants the 260-million light receivers that you have to operate at 'full bore' in order to let in *all* the information that so appeals to you.

It is the same for all your other senses.

When you Love, or are in Love, your entire body and sensory system 'opens out' and lets much more information from the Universe flood in. You become, in the true meaning of the phrase, '*open-minded*'. You are immediately in a state in which your learning, memory, concentration, focus and ability to respond are all enhanced, revealing your full potential and power to you.

True power is not the ability momentarily to impose your will upon another person or other people – there is no inner, long-term security in that kind of power. As time changes that power will change (and diminish) too.

True power is also not simply having a strong body that makes you physically dominant over others. Time will change this too. All such 'physical powers' are temporary, and if they have been your mainstay, the absence or loss of them can lead to fear and massive insecurity.

Real power lies in the Power of Love, as evidenced throughout history by single individuals such as Buddha, Jesus and Muhammad. The mighty armies and worldly leaders of their time are long forgotten. But the memories of those mighty spirits who fought with the Power of Love are still flowering in an increasing number of human souls.

And this love can 'move mountains', prompting ordinary people to quite extraordinary feats – the mother who lifts a car up to release her child pinned underneath, or the father who digs with his bare hands to free his son trapped under a mudslide.

suffering the loss of a loved one

One of the greatest sufferings we can experience is that of the loss of love, and especially the loss of a particularly cherished family member or friend.

The loss is devastating, and can feel unbearable.

This pain and suffering *can* be eased, however, by understanding the 'Big Picture' and by becoming more aware of others and *their* own situation. This is beautifully illustrated by a story from the life of Buddha.

One day Kisa Gotami came to Buddha crying, 'O Exalted One, my only son has died. I went to everyone and asked, "Is there no medicine to bring my son back to life?" And they replied, "There is no medicine; but go to the Exalted One, he may be able to help you." Can you, O Exalted One, give me medicine to bring my only son back to life?'

Looking at her with compassion, Buddha replied, 'You did well, Kisa Gotami, in coming here for medicine. Go, and bring me for medicine some tiny grains of mustard seed from every house where no one – neither parent, child, relative, nor servant – has died.'

Kisa Gotami, delighted in her heart, went away to fetch as many tiny grains of mustard seed as she could find. From one house to another, she searched frantically all day long, and each time she was told, 'Alas! Great is the count of the dead in this house.'

Overcome with exhaustion, she finally said, 'My dear little boy, I thought you alone had been overtaken by this thing which men call death. But now I see that you are not the only one, for this is a law common to all mankind.'

Suffering is common to all of us. When suffering such loss of Love, it is important to try to direct that 'energy of loss' not into a negative spiral of self-pity and depression, but into a positive spiral of understanding, care and compassion. Below is the extraordinary story of one woman who was finally able to make sense of her loss of Love, and had the strength to use that hard-gained knowledge to help other people in similar situations.

'Dying for Loss of Love'

I was once introduced to a woman who was 'dying for loss of love'.

She and her husband had been on a cross-Channel ferry that had sunk with horrific loss of life. She had been one of the survivors; her husband had died.

For 10 years she had been unable to 'face' the situation; or, more accurately, to face the horror of the monstrous memories that kept lurching out of the blackness at her whenever her mind was about to rest.

For years she had been going to 'experts', trying to get rid of those memories. I explained to her that it was impossible to 'get rid' of a memory unless you excised part of your brain! The only way to deal with it successfully was to embrace it and use it.

I asked her to be courageous and look again at what had actually happened. Having done this, she would then hopefully be able to deal with the tragedy more appropriately, and to use it to her life-long advantage rather than reducing herself to a shattered wreck. She was both courageous and committed, and within a short time was reliving the entire event.

When the ship started sinking, she found her husband singing Irish ballads, downing Guinness and saying, sincerely and very happily: 'What a wonderful way to go!' All around her people were panicking; many yelling: 'It's all over.' 'Oh my God, we're finished.' 'We're going to die.' 'There's no hope.' Her own reaction was to *live*! She said to her husband, 'Come on' (he didn't), and then made for the nearest exit.

Through all the panic and confusion, she made a beeline for where she knew the lifeboats were, and seeing that they were all afloat, dived into the water and made straight for one. Clambering aboard with the other few survivors, she observed, over the next horrible hour, that nearly all those who had made it to the lifeboats had had a singular desire to survive, and had committed themselves to saving their lives and others' too.

All those who had died, she noticed with a shudder, had in some way 'given up' well before the last moment. By reliving the horror of what she had been through, she came to realize that her husband had not been afraid of death, and that she herself had survived such a terrible life-threatening situation through her own extraordinary spirit and will to live.

Eventually she was able to use these precious insights to help others to understand their own fears, and to overcome their own life-devastating events. In turn, this allowed her to regain some peace and sense of purpose herself.

the story of the prisoners on death row

At the end of the last century an investigative journalist in America did an extraordinary survey: she asked the librarians in state prisons to give her feedback on what kind of books prisoners on Death Row were reading in the year before their execution date.

the power of spiritual intelligence

From the following list of subjects, pick the one you think was, by far, the most popular:

- The Bible and other religious texts
- Books on law
- Adventure stories
- Pornography
- Poetry
- Philosophy
- Biographies
- How to write love letters and poetry
- Astronomy
- Great escapes
- Cartoon books
- Joke books
- Communication books

To everyone's amazement, easily the most popular were books on how to write love poetry and love letters.

In the darkest moments of life, even those condemned as 'animals' and 'scum of the earth' had Love as their prime focus of attention, and the expression of their Love as their life's last Vision and intent.

It is now time for you to exercise the infinite Spiritual muscle-power of your Love.

spiritual workout

1 Allow Yourself to Love

In our post-industrial, information age, where money is regarded as power and a frantically busy life a sign of success, emotions, and especially Love, are frowned upon and considered 'wimpish'. We tend to downgrade or unnecessarily inhibit and restrict ourselves in this area.

Now that you more fully realize that real strength and heroism lies not in material or physical strength, but in Spiritual love and compassion, concentrate on boosting this aspect of your personal power. It can bring you infinite rewards.

2 Express Your Grief

As with showing compassion and Love, expressions of grief in much of modern society are considered weak. This is wrong. Expressing grief is a sign of *strength*.

We all feel pain. To 'hold it in' is not strong – it is ridiculous and counterproductive! Have a good cry, and don't be afraid to show your pain and grief.

One most useful way to express grief or pain, I find, is through writing, especially short poems. Such brief writings serve the purpose of expressing, releasing and capturing those moments of 'love-in-pain', and then allow me to move on.

3 Be Aware of Others' Sufferings

As we saw with the story of Kisa Gotami, all people suffer. The older you are, the more likelihood there is that you will have experienced major tragedies, pain and suffering in your life – illnesses or the deaths of loved ones.

Upgrade your 'Compassion Engine' and look more searchingly into the eyes of your travelling companions on Planet Earth. When you understand more deeply their own life stories, you will be able to embrace them more easily with Understanding and Love.

'Love gives naught but itself and takes naught
from itself.
Love possess not nor would it be possessed,
For love is sufficient unto love.'

(Kahlil Gibran)

4 Be More Understanding of Your Own Suffering

When 'bad' or 'negative' things happen to people, there is often a wail of: 'Why me?'; 'It's not fair!'; 'It always happens to me!'; 'I always have bad luck!'

The simple truth about these exclamations is that nearly *everybody* says them! In other words, once again, you are not alone. *Everybody* is in the same boat!

You belong to a global community.

Rather than focusing on your own despair, bad luck or misfortune, use it to reach out to all those other millions of people who are suffering, just like you.

5 Use Your 'Bad' Experiences for Good

Everything that has happened to you in your life or that you have done is part of your history and your life story. Remember the story of the lady and the boat, and realize that all your 'negative' or 'bad' experiences are special events that are unique to you. You can use them to help others either avoid or deal with the same kind of mistakes/tragedies as you have experienced. The proper use of the full range of your life's experiences is known as Wisdom.

Use your life knowledge well, and you will become Wise.

6 Love Yourself

Love yourself. It is only when you have learnt to love and respect yourself, that you can begin to love and respect other people.

Many of the problems people face in their lives can be traced back to a lack of love for themselves. Addictions to substances such as caffeine, nicotine, alcohol, or other drugs, for example, are a case in point.

If you are struggling to give up an addiction, bring your Power of Love to bear. Focus on your own magnificence, the miracle and uniqueness of who you are, your Vision and your infinite potential, and expand that bubble of Love on a daily basis. As it grows, the 'space' given to the addiction will gradually be squeezed out, and your body and mind will be free as they should be.

7 Become More Involved with Animals

Make sure you live with, play with and Love animals.

Animals, especially the higher vertebrates, experience the emotions of pain, grief and love much as we do. Researchers have also found that those who have pets live more emotionally stable, happy and loving lives. Think of the unmitigated joy and affection of a dog when it meets its long-absent owner, and learn from this kind of expression of Love how to express it yourself!

8 Spread the Word!

Make sure, every day, that you tell someone that you Love them. Every day find other ways to express your Love for others.

9 Do Exactly the Same for Yourself!

Here is a visualization practice to enhance your love and self-love.

Imagine someone who has loved you in the past. Recollect the feeling of being completely and utterly accepted for yourself. This person could be a family member, a friend, lover or a divine being. Visualize that person looking at you with love. Allow that feeling to penetrate your body. Really allow yourself to accept the love. Bask in it for five minutes.

You will find that when you stir and go back into the everyday world you will feel compelled to share this love with others.

10 A Loving-Kindness Meditation

Sit in a quiet, comfortable spot. Relax and breathe out. Then picture your most dearly loved ones.

Allow your feelings of love to increase; remember how wonderful they are and how grateful you are to have them in your life. They can be people from your past or your present, alive or dead. Stay connected to your feelings of great love for a few minutes.

Next, turn your attention to people you like; they could be colleagues, neighbours, casual acquaintances. Try to extend the same love and concern to them as you would to your dearly loved ones. Recognize that like all other beings, they want to achieve happiness and peace. Allow the space in your heart for these feelings of love and concern for your acquaintances to grow.

Then, turn your attention to those toward whom you feel neutral. They can be people you see on the train on the way to work or people you may see in the supermarket. Again try to extend your feelings of love to them and concern that they, too, find happiness and relief from suffering, and that their friends and family do likewise. Spend some time doing this.

Last, and most difficult, picture your enemies: the person who backstabbed you at work, an ex who behaved badly, someone who bullied your child. Try to see them as people who, like yourself, want their sufferings to end and want to experience happiness. Try to extend love to them. Keep practising. The ideal is eventually to be able to extend the same kind of care and concern to everyone.

spirit boosters

- I am a Loving person.
- Love is my guiding star.
- I use my own suffering to become wise, compassionate and charitable towards others.
- I am calm and courageous in the face of adversity.
- I regularly tell those closest to me how much I appreciate and Love them.

all you need is love!

'Some day, after we have mastered the winds, the waves, the tides, and gravity, we shall harness the energies of love. Then, for the second time in the history of the world, humankind will have discovered fire.'

(Teilhard de Chardin)

Stay focused on the Big Picture. Value yourself and constantly hone your personal ethical principles. Keep your Life Vision constantly as a beacon in front of you. Be Compassionate and Understanding towards yourself and others. Become increasingly Grateful and Charitable. Laugh and let the world laugh with you. Continue to release the child within you. Grow your inner strength through the Power of Ritual. Create both inner and outer Peace.

Through these actions you will develop, possess, realize and share the Power of Love.

If you want to learn more about Creative Intelligence, and to take part in games, quizzes and discussions around all of the subjects covered here, why don't you visit

www.Mind-Map.com

or contact Tony at the Buzan Centre:

Buzan Centres Ltd
54 Parkstone Road
Poole, Dorset BH15 2PG
Tel: +44 (0) 1202 674676
Fax: +44 (0) 1202 674776

Buzan Centers Inc. (Americas)
PO Box 4
Palm Beach
FL 33480
USA
Tel: +1 561 881 0188
Fax: +1 561 434 1682

Or email: Buzan@Mind-Map.com